PHILOSOPHIC REFLECTIONS ON

Liberty
and
Democracy

Edited by
Tibor R. Machan

HOOVER INSTITUTION PRESS

Stanford University   Stanford, California

www.hoover.org

Hoover Institution Press Publication No. 504

First printing 2002
08 07 06 05 04 03 02   9 8 7 6 5 4 3 2 1

Manufactured in the United States of America
The paper used in this publication meets the minimum requirements
of American National Standard for Information Sciences—Permanence
of Paper for Printed Library Materials, ANSI Z39.48-1984. ♾

Library of Congress Cataloging-in-Publication Data
Liberty and democracy / edited by Tibor R. Machan.
     p.   cm.
Includes bibliographical references and index.
ISBN 0-8179-2922-3
    1. Democracy.   2. Liberty.   I. Machan, Tibor R.
JC423 .L5178   2002
321.8—dc21   2002027326

Democracy without constitutional liberalism is not simply inadequate, but dangerous, bringing with it the erosion of liberty, the abuse of power, ethnic divisions, and even war. Eighty years ago, Woodrow Wilson took America into the twentieth century with a challenge, to make the world safe for democracy. As we approach the next century, our task is to make democracy safe for the world.

Fareed Zakaria
"The Rise of Illiberal Democracy"

CONTENTS

ACKNOWLEDGMENTS

ONCE AGAIN I wish to express my gratitude to the Hoover Institution on War, Revolution and Peace and its director, John Raisian, for supporting the publication of this work. Joanne and her late husband, Johan Blokker, gave generously in support of the Hoover Institution Press series, Philosophic Reflections on a Free Society, for which I wish to express my deep gratitude. The contributing authors were cooperative, patient, and conscientious throughout the entire publishing process. David M. Brown has helped with some editing, and I wish to thank him for this. Tina Garcia has been very helpful with administrative aspects of this project, and, once again, the diligence of Pat Baker, Ann Wood, and Marshall Blanchard of the Hoover Institution Press is also much appreciated.

CONTRIBUTORS

JOHN HOSPERS is emeritus professor of philosophy, University of Southern California. He is the author of *Understanding the Arts*, *Meaning and Truth in the Arts*, *Introduction to Philosophical Analysis*, and *Human Conduct* (the latter two were revised in 1996). He has also compiled four anthologies and published 200 essays in philosophical, aesthetic, and political journals.

GREGORY R. JOHNSON has an M.A. and a Ph.D. in philosophy from the Catholic University of America in Washington, D.C., and teaches philosophy at the Pacific School of Religion in Berkeley, California. He is the author of articles on modern philosophy (focusing on Kant, Swedenborg, and Rousseau), as well as on figures and topics in contemporary continental philosophy, moral and political philosophy, and philosophy and literature.

NEERA K. BADHWAR is an associate professor of philosophy, University of Oklahoma. She has published extensively in ethics and on the philosophy of Aristotle.

LOREN E. LOMASKY is a professor of philosophy, Bowling Green

State University, Ohio. He is author of *Persons, Rights, and the Moral Community*.

TIBOR R. MACHAN is Distinguished Fellow and Freedom Communications Professor of Business Ethics and Free Enterprise at the Leatherby Center for Entrepreneurship and Business Ethics, Argyros School of Business and Economics, Chapman University, and a Research Fellow at the Hoover Institution.

The
Democratic
Ideal

Tibor R. Machan

THESE DAYS almost everybody believes in democracy. But not everybody agrees on just what democracy is.

Literally, the term means "the rule of the people." *Demos* is Greek for "people," and *kratos* is Greek for strength or power, derivatively, "rule." Hence, democracy empowers the people to rule.

Yet this etymological excursion hardly settles the matter, for there remains the question of what exactly constitutes "the people." The concept could simply be a shorthand way of referring to everyone individually. Or it could refer to an entity that comprises all these individuals but that is somehow greater than the sum of the parts and possessive of a life unto itself.[1]

In the days following the 2000 U.S. presidential election, when much of America was on pins and needles over the issue of the electoral count in Florida, there was a good deal of rhetoric about "the will of the people." Political partisans ap-

---

1. Even though "the people" could be used to mean all the individuals in some country or other grouping, it is possible to speak of "the interest of the people" or "the good of the people" and so refer to some supposed *common* interest or good, one shared by all individuals.

peared on television to tell us they wanted to make sure the electoral process accurately expressed "the will of the people." By this they apparently meant that they wanted an accurate accounting of how the majority of voters had in fact voted. But does such an accounting really inform us of the "will of the people"? And even if it does, are candidates then obliged to enact this transcribed "will of the people," whatever that is supposed to be, once they take office?

It all depends. If "the people" designates some entity over and above the individuals who compose it, then this entity may indeed possess a single will of some kind or another, and it may indeed be vital for us to know what this will is.[2] But it may not be a good idea to always obey this alleged will. We know, for example, that lynching an accused person and supporting an inhumane institution, such as slavery, are just plain wrong even if such choices are the will of the majority. Even if they make those choices democratically, via their votes. Democracy cannot supersede ethics. It is not beyond good and evil.

The necessity of constraining the majority from doing wrong is an underlying principle of the Bill of Rights. If each particular individual who is a constituent of "the people" has rights, he has those rights even if most of his neighbors are eager to violate them; therefore, they may be institutionally prevented from so violating them. A right is a constraint on others. If that constraint is justified, it's justified no matter how large the number of those others happens to be. As the Declaration of Indepen-

---

2. There is, of course, Rousseau's doctrine of general will, but this refers, essentially, to an ideal desire to promote the common good, and that common good may well be very different from what the majority of voters desire and could actually amount to something very minimal, such as protection of everyone's right to liberty. For a very interesting and thorough discussion, see Bernard Bonsanquet, *The Philosophical Theory of the State and Other Essays* (South Bend, Ind.: St. Augustine's Press, 1998).

dence puts the matter, certain individual rights—among them the rights to life, liberty, and the pursuit of happiness—are unalienable, meaning that no justification exists for ignoring and violating them. Governments are instituted among men precisely in order to secure those rights.

Now compare this idea to what many take "the will of the people" to mean: that nearly anything the majority of voters decides at the ballot booth is ipso facto sacrosanct. It is right if the people vote for taxpayer-funded prescription drugs for the elderly; right if the people vote to stop gays and lesbians from marrying; right if the people vote to stop tax dollars from being used for private schools; right if the people vote to empower representatives to impose a military draft or a civil ban on alcohol use; the examples are endless.

All these so-called public policies violate the unalienable rights of some individuals—less drastically than lynching or slavery do, to be sure, but not all that much less drastically than theft or battery or kidnapping. Yet many think the "will of the people" somehow justifies such actions.

Actually, of course, there is no such unitary will, only the highly disparate individual choices and values of all the individual members of a society. Properly employed, "the people," or society, is only a shortcut term for designating the total number of these individuals, not some kind of greater organism of which those individuals are mere cells. There may well be but very few items that can count as *the* (united) will of the people. They would have to be matters that everyone in society agrees upon, at least implicitly—for example, the minimal standards of civilized behavior that one needs to follow in order to be a member of society at all.

Protection from molestation and violence is something we could arguably all be presumed to want as citizens of a country. But because a commitment to having our rights respected, secured, and protected does not imply the loss of our sovereignty, the "will of the people" in that very limited sense cannot be said to sanction the kind of unlimited democracy that many societies approximate. These were the kinds of concerns the founders of the United States and, less consistently, the framers of the Constitution probably had in mind when the country was established. They wanted to put on record that the purpose of government is to secure our individual rights, period. Under a rule of individual rights, what voters could do would be tightly constrained. Mostly it would be limited to the selection of officials.

One reason we regard democracy as a just mode of political decision making is that we believe citizens properly possess ultimate authority over certain matters in the polis. They possess this ultimate authority because, as adults, they have an equal stake in *their* political institutions, laws, public policies, foreign relations, and so on. Another reason we favor democracy is the view that there may be wisdom in great numbers—50 million Frenchman can't be wrong, can they? Well, maybe they can, but perhaps the forum afforded by large numbers does tend to promote political temperance and prudence.

That claim, that all members of a community enjoy an equal status with respect to their citizenship, hinges in turn on certain extrapolitical or prepolitical matters to be discerned by way of reflecting on human nature and proper human relations. This equal status arguably arises, in the end, from the moral fact that each individual adult human being's most fundamental task of life is to flourish as a rational animal. Because adults can achieve this goal only if they are not involuntarily subject to the will of another—in which case, that other's choices would be the ruling element—they must be sovereign in their communities. From this it follows that they may not be denied a say in their own political fate. Ergo, they have a civic right to a system of government that permits such a say, that is, democracy.

The most prominent ancient political philosophers tended to reject democracy in favor of some kind of aristocracy based on a hierarchical understanding of human society. Persons deemed naturally superior to others would have a special right to rule. This way of thinking—never fully embraced by all those who reflected on political matters—was gradually abandoned, especially in the modern era, with the advent of the political theory of Thomas Hobbes.

Within the Hobbesian framework—though not within the mind of Hobbes himself, who supported absolute monarchy—democracy can be recommended on materialist grounds. Insofar as we are all nothing but bits of matter in motion, we lack any significant, fundamental differentiating attributes that would make some humans superior to others.[3] Even our so-called human nature is merely nominal,[4] a category concocted by the human intellect's automatic response to the motions affecting the brain, a response motivated by the drive for self-preservation. We are able to remain in continued motion in part by naming groups of impulses affecting the brain.[5] So the reason for democracy by way of a Hobbesian approach is that nothing justifies differentiating some people from others. Indeed, if one were to be fully consistent, nothing at the metaphysical, fundamental level of being justifies differentiating anything from anything else whatever. One can't get very far in the real world, let alone in a moral argument, with this kind

---

3. Although the philosophical position that underlies Hobbes's politics would support democratic government, Hobbes himself believed that only an absolute monarch, albeit elected by all, would suffice for purposes of keeping the peace and advancing the well-being of all members of a society.

4. "Nominal" here means "common meaning in name only."

5. Thomas Hobbes, *Leviathan*, ed. Michael Oakshott (New York: Collier Books, 1972).

of view, but it does underlie a certain egalitarian rationale for democracy.

A somewhat different rationale arises from the Lockean view. According to Locke—at least when we turn to his political treatise—we are all equal (in having a moral nature) and independent (without legal obligations to anyone) in the state of nature, that is, prior to the formation of or apart from civil society or the polis.[6] In Locke's view, which explicitly endorses a certain measure of democracy, a democratic approach to political decision making is justified because we have basic rights that imply that if we are to be governed, our consent is required.

A more theological take on this would be to claim that we are all equally precious children of God. As such, it is only just that here on Earth our political institutions require that each of us be consulted on how society ought to be governed. This view is compatible with Locke's even if one prefers to understand his arguments in purely secular terms.

In the Lockean perspective, we are all moral agents, obliged to live up to our moral responsibilities, and in this respect, we are all alike. Our natural rights spell out, for each of us, a sphere of sovereignty or personal authority or jurisdiction in which we are able to function as moral agents. Leaving aside tricky borderline cases of defective or incapacitated persons, there are no natural masters or natural slaves. If these facts are kept in clear focus, one will realize that a just human community can regard no one as intrinsically superior or inferior regarding the issue of the authority to make law and to govern. Thus, democracy.

---

6. It is usually noted that Locke has in mind a fictional or a hypothetical state of nature only. Yet, arguably, Locke may well have had some historical states of human affairs in mind, such as those of nomadic and unorganized assemblies of human beings. It is also possible to consider some areas of human inhabitation—areas that are removed from civil government, like the high seas or even city back alleys—as Lockean states of nature.

In this light, democracy is morally required by the right to take part in political decisions and the right to give consent to governance. It is our natural right to person and estate that warrants our right to political participation. But the democratic process cannot be applied to everything under the sun one might want to influence. That is to say, democracy has a proper *sphere*.

Clearly, some disagree. Some do believe (at least some of the time) that democracy should be unlimited and all that matters is whether "the people" will things to be one way versus another way. Even some interpreters of Locke, for example, Wilmore Kendall and his followers, as well as some recent conservatives, for example, Robert Bork, have dared to claim this.[7] They argue that once human beings have emerged from a state of nature, they have in effect adopted democracy as a decision-making process regarding whatever comes up for public discussion.

It is hardly clear that Locke can be coherently interpreted this way, but in any case, the assumption of unlimited democracy is wrongheaded. For in Locke, the justification for government lies in the need to protect our natural rights, a protection not easily obtained (except by the strong) in the state of nature.[8] Because establishing, maintaining, and protecting our rights is

7. Among those on the Left, the work of Benjamin Barker, *Strong Democracy* (Berkeley, Calif.: University of California Press, 1990), stands out as a sustained argument for the priority of democracy over other considerations. Others, too, have stressed this, among them Richard Rorty and Jurgen Habermas.

8. The state of nature need not be a source of much intellectual consternation. It refers to any circumstance not governed by due process or the rule of law, one we may encounter even today, in a back alley or any place distant from civilization and its protections. That was the situation in the classic Western movie *The Man Who Shot Liberty Valance* before John Wayne enabled James Stewart to establish law and order.

itself a human activity that can be done well or badly, it, too, must be guided by principles—by due process—including those of our natural rights. Government may not encroach upon those rights lest its proper purpose be undermined in the name of achieving it. Perhaps the best way to understand this is in terms of the commonsense notion that even the securing of highly valued goals does not justify the employment of immoral means.

In any case, unless the people express and implement their will as they should, democracy without being guided by norms can itself become self-defeating. Unlimited democracy can undo democracy itself. This is just what happened in the Weimar Republic, for example, as Adolf Hitler was voted into power by people who felt entitled to demand anything and everything via politics. Once he had consolidated his power the führer proceeded to scotch democracy altogether.

That's an extreme example, but there are less severe instances of the same implosive process in our own history. Suppose Americans democratically vote to exclude some people from the voting process—linking the right to vote to, say, education, wealth, race, or some other prerequisite—as has been done at one time or another at both the federal and state levels. Then the democratic process is distorted. The same distortion occurs when the federal government essays to be so generously "inclusive" of some hitherto-neglected minority groups that it awards a lower level of representation to members of other groups. Notwithstanding the purported good intentions, the policy violates the equal rights of individuals to take part in the political process.

The underlying justification for democracy is that individuals have the right to consent to their government. But to the extent that the democratic process produces governmental measures that violate their natural rights, the capacity of these rights-holding individuals to be equally free, full participants in the democratic process is undermined.

Related problems abound when democracy is not properly limited in scope. If by the democratic process the rights to life, liberty, or property could be abrogated or violated, some or many participants in democracy would no longer be able to act freely and independently. The majority could threaten such participants and their free judgments, even enact measures that would authorize vindictive official actions against them. Democracy becomes an empty shell. Thus were the so-called democracies of the former Soviet bloc a complete farce despite the vast numbers of those who participated. The citizenry could not vote as they wanted, for whom they wanted.

Once a system of laws is in place, if democracy is too loose and unrestricted in its scope, not only is the situation unjust in and of itself, but it also spawns unwelcome paradoxes for the voter. If when I vote I know that voting my conscience may result in having my sovereignty undermined or my property confiscated—in my being partially enslaved—I will probably not vote my conscience. I will act like the victim of the mugger upon hearing "Your money or your life!" When I hand over my money, I do it under compulsion, not by choice; my acquiescence does not express the will that I would exercise if I were not being threatened.

It is a myth that we always have a free choice, for a "choice" that is set out by others and that robs one of prospects for a self-governed future is not a free but a highly constrained, coerced choice. (Indeed, it is not so much a choice as a selection from a list of options imposed by others.) If a democratic process allows this to happen, those who reject the rights-violating outcome of voting can vote only under severe constraint.

Arguably, some version of democracy is required if a legal system is to be established at all, even an anarchist one, because before decent laws can be instituted or established, they require serious support.[9] If that support is given by a solid enough majority, it may (a) resist rejection by many who might hesitate but see benefit in the association and (b) set into motion a lasting and stable (and, perhaps, entirely noncoercive) legal order.

But even in such a legal order it is possible that some citizens will want to enact public policies that do not enjoy unanimous support. If justice requires *full* consent of the governed—not merely consent of the governed in the sense conferred by a majority of those who vote—then such policies may not be imposed, except with regard to formal or procedural matters necessary to democratic functioning as such.

We can extend these concerns to the realm of contemporary politics in Western democracies. Let's focus on the general situation in the United States of America today.

It is telling that certain checks on the "will of the people" are widely recognized and accepted even by those who toss the notion around fairly confidently. For example, whenever funding for public programs is being cut, those whose benefits are being reduced protest that their needs are not being properly met. This amounts to criticizing the results of the democratic process, such as it is, despite its democratic character. Thus, even those who directly benefit from the systematic violation of the rights of others can see that democratic processes aren't enough, per se, to warrant democratic outcomes. Rather, they can be evaluated with respect to an ethical standard that exists apart from democratic norms as such.

On the other hand, when new public programs or new funding of old programs are given democratic endorsement, clearly

9. I have in mind here a kind of anarchism that does not abolish law but makes it entirely a matter of private provision. See, for example, Bruce Benson's *The Enterprise of Law* (San Francisco: Pacific Research Institute for Public Policy, 1990).

diminishing the well-being of those who must pay for them with higher taxes, the same crew contends that inasmuch as this wealth transference is simply the result of democracy, any complaints must be unjustified. As the point is usually put: "We" have decided to fund social security, unemployment compensation, the national parks, public broadcasting, or whatnot—haven't we?

If the results of democratic process are per se justified, how can it be okay to violate the individual rights to liberty and property of millions of people merely because "we" have democratically decided to do so but not okay to trim the benefits of handout recipients if a somewhat differently configured lot of us decide, democratically, to do that? The contradiction can't be genuinely resolved, but it is often argued that in those cases where the outcomes aren't the desired outcomes, something in the democratic process must have "gone wrong." People must have been hoodwinked or been suffering from a false consciousness that impaired their judgment when they entered the polling booth.[10]

In point of fact, for most of those who support what has come to be called strong democracy, democracy is merely a convenient path to the redistribution of wealth, a handy means of transforming plain theft into bland and dignified public policy. That's why, when democracy produces a result that hampers such redistribution, democratic themes are suddenly inadequate.

What is true is that there must *always* be some specification

10. This is duplicity. If Republicans, for example, elect to cut federal programs that leave open the possibility that some states will not spend money on poor children's lunches, that is supposed to be mean-minded, cruel, and morally insidious. But if Democrats decide to increase taxes for various programs that intrude on the liberty of various citizens, all's well that end's well.

of the goals for which democracy is appropriate if democracy itself is to be justified. Sometimes the majority does right, sometimes wrong. The task of political theory is, in part, to identify those areas of public life that should be subject to democratic decision making and those that should be permanently and irremediably exempt from it.

The answer "Well, it was done democratically, so don't sweat it" is, then, no answer to those who protest the abducting of their lifetime or life-products by majority vote. The goal of democracy cannot be the facilitation of theft. Whether alone or in concert with a gang, there are some things a human being simply may not do to other human beings. In particular, no one may take—or take over—another's life. This is so whether the other in question is beautiful, rich, and talented or solitary, poor, nasty, and brutish. Neither the fortunate nor the unfortunate may be exploited by others without consent. And the fact that under democracy the numbers of those who do such things is greater and may even constitute a majority of those concerned makes not a whit of moral difference; nor does the fact that some definite procedures are followed as these rights-violating policies are imposed. Without at least the implicit consent of those who are to be deprived, any such process is invalid and unjust.

None of this should be taken to imply, of course, that widespread callousness toward the unfortunate is okay; only that the remedy must be moral suasion and the example of one's own personal conduct. To be generous to those in need requires not a law, and not a gun, but a personal choice.

When members of a society learn that moral and political principles may not be violated by the democratic process—that they may not violate anyone's rights with the excuse that "we" did it, so it's okay—they also learn that doing the right thing has to be a matter of voluntary choice. So the help that the poor and needy should be given must be given on the initiative of the free citizen, via charity and philanthropy, whether individual or organized. Democracy may not trump individual rights.

However extreme this perspective may seem at first glance, it is no more than the application of the principle of due process—so well recognized in some parts of the law—to all human relationships.

In his book on classical liberalism, Ludwig von Mises hails the free society precisely for its absence of pomp.[11] The free society can do without the trappings of passion and feeling, he says; all it needs is the endorsement of argument or dispassionate reason. He was only half right.

Cold reason does support the free society. But we can, and should, also feel enthusiasm for its supreme value. As Henry Hazlitt, another champion of liberty, puts it: "The superior freedom of the capitalist system, its superior justice, and its superior productivity are not three superiorities, but one. The justice follows from the freedom and the productivity follows from the freedom and the justice."[12]

In the pages that follow, contributors grapple with the issue of the proper role of democracy in a community that is committed to respecting and protecting the unalienable individual rights of all members. It is clear that something salutary is

---

11. "No sect and no political party has believed that it could afford to forgo advancing its cause by appealing to men's senses. Rhetorical bombast, music, and song resound, banners wave, flowers and colors serve as symbols, and the leaders seek to attach their followers to their own person. Liberalism has nothing to do with all this. It has no party flower and no party color, no party song and no party idols, no symbols and no slogans. It has the substance and the arguments. These must lead it to victory." Ludwig von Mises, *Liberalism*, German ed. Latest English edition, Irvington, N.Y.: The Foundation for Economic Education, 1985. Translation by Ralph Raico. Online edition, The Mises Institute, © 2000.

12. Henry Hazlitt, quoted in *The Freeman* (June 1993): 225.

involved when a society is democratic rather than dictatorial or despotic. What exactly this is, and how it meshes with a free society's uncompromising support of individual sovereignty, is the focus of this volume.

CHAPTER ONE

Default and Dynamic Democracy

Loren E. Lomasky

1989 WAS SIGNIFICANT for the iconography of politics. Coincidentally, two of its memorable moments involved walls. One, the Berlin Wall, which for a generation stood as an ugly gash across the center of Europe, came down amidst joyous celebration and an outpouring of long-deferred optimism for the future. The other, the Democracy Wall, went up in Beijing's Tiananmen Square, with similar optimism. Both wall and optimism proved short-lived, however—the tanks and troops of the gerontocracy soon pounded it into bits even smaller than those to which its Berlin cousin had been reduced. Distinct outcomes, but the aspiration common to both was democracy.

The American presidential election of 2000 afforded other memorable images. It was the year that the term *chad* conspicuously entered the national vocabulary, usually modified by *hanging* or *pregnant*. Florida voters in remarkable number showed themselves flummoxed by two-column ballots the design of which was less complicated than the golf scorecards they easily maintain. Editorialists pontificated concerning whether what really should matter were votes as cast or the votes that people believed they were casting. Spokespersons for the two candidates formulated transparently self-serving moral and legal rationales as to why their man should be the next president. Selection of the administration that would govern the world's most powerful nation hinged on accident, confusion, and happenstance, displaying all the randomness of a Lucky-7 lottery drawing. This, too, is a recognizable image of democracy.

The contrast suggests numerous questions. How much moral weight is borne by occasional trips to the polls of citizens who can barely distinguish among the candidates and issues? If, as has been said, war is politics by other means, then is not majority rule essentially a way of carrying out that struggle by counting noses rather than casualties? What, after all, is so special about democracy?

The great liberal thinkers of the tradition offer precious little help. John Locke in *The Second Treatise of Government* was the first to issue the pivotal announcement that all human beings possess basic rights to life, liberty, and property and that governments are instituted to vindicate those rights. But as social life does not admit of the precision of mathematics, difficulties in governance will arise that do not admit of algorithmic decision procedures. Because practical quandaries demand some resolution or other, there is need for a means to cut through uncertainties and disagreement. That is why the citizenry creates a legislative body to deliberate on its behalf, after which it says yea or nay. Because the ship of state must move in one direction or the other, it is only reasonable, claims Locke, that it should incline toward the larger number.[1]

1. "For when any number of men have, by the consent of their every individual, made a community, they have thereby made that community one body, with a power to act as one body, which is only by the will and determination of the majority; for that which acts any community being only the consent of the individuals of it, and it being necessary to that which is one body to move one way, it is necessary the body should move that way whither

The only thing special about majorities is that they are not minorities. To them, crucially, is imputed no greater share of virtue or deputation to act as God's viceroy on Earth. On the contrary, their edicts are to be tightly constrained by attention to the antecedent rights of individuals and by procedures that separate powers and otherwise put various stumbling blocks in the way of potentially tyrannous usurpations. These Lockean themes were taken up by his successors. On this side of the Atlantic, they include the Declaration of Independence and the Constitution. Within this tradition, liberty is primary, democracy distinctly secondary. What this potted history leaves unexplained, however, is democracy's capacity to serve as an ideal prompting celebration at one extreme and martyrdom at the other. The aim of this essay is to make some progress toward supplying an answer.

Section 1 briefly examines contemporary descendants of Lockean majoritarianism. They are found to be serviceable enough but without much resonance in the political imagination. Section 2 introduces the chief rival conception of democracy, one tracing back to Jean Jacques Rousseau. There's no denying it is laden with romance, but its credentials as a practical basis for collective decision making are suspect. The contrast suggests that democrats can have their realism or have their idealism but not both. Section 3 opposes that suggestion with a model featuring individuals who are every bit as hard-headed when donning the persona of citizen as they are in their capacity as economic agents, yet who respond to different motivations as they move from market to voting booth. Section 4 draws out

---

the greater force carries it, which is the consent of the majority; or else it is impossible it should act or continue one body, one community, which the consent of every individual that united into it agreed that it should; and so every one is bound by that consent to be concluded by the majority." Locke, *The Second Treatise of Government*, §96.

some implications for the normative status of democratic institutions.

I. DEFAULT DEMOCRACY

Democracy is, definitionally, rule of the *demos*, the people, the many. Spelling out how that is supposed to work is problematic. An alternative approach proceeds by noting what democracy is *not*. Specifically, it is not the exercise of governance by one authoritative monarch, ruling class, committee of oligarches, or clerisy. Holding periodic elections for the purpose of shuffling out the old occupants of parliaments and presidential suites and replacing them with a new crowd does not guarantee steady moral improvement, let alone wise rule by a statesmanlike elite. But what it usually does manage to achieve is some check to ambition. Even if replacements of officeholders were entirely at random, the fact of alteration by itself stands in the way of erecting and indefinitely maintaining potentially tyrannous fiefdoms. What is important in this conception is not so much *who* rules, although it need not be denied that the character of officeholders can make an appreciable difference for political outcomes, but that governance is shaken up at irregular intervals.

Compared with classical models of political order, this one is not particularly lofty. Certainly it falls far short of the administration of Plato's Republic by philosopher-kings who know the common good, are reliably motivated by concern for it, and possess expertise sufficient to achieve it. Aristotle and Cicero offer somewhat more down-to-earth scenarios of rule by the wise and virtuous, but as in the story told by Plato, the regimes that secure their endorsements feature governance by the best and brightest for the sake of all. The stories these classical authors tell are indeed edifying, but one can't avoid the suspicion that their genre is at least as much fantasy as philosophy.

If we had a reliable source of supply for philosopher-kings or benevolent despots, then the case for democracy would be much less persuasive. Practice reveals, however, that these are always in short supply. Those who most vociferously nominate themselves for such standing usually prove to be abject pretenders. Even if we were in possession of some reliable procedure for identifying those most fit to rule, preserving that fitness is a further and, arguably, intractable task. Lord Acton noted, "Power tends to corrupt and absolute power corrupts absolutely." To pick only one example from numerous contenders, the presidential pardons issued during the last hours of the Clinton administration indicate that the dawning of the twenty-first century has not rendered Acton's famous dictum any less salient. Philosopher-kings are more apt to become addicted to the appurtenances of kingly status than to remain devoted to the quiet charms of philosophical reflection; the autocrat's despotism is likely to outlive his benevolence.

So for democracy to win the political prize, its credentials need not be altogether glittering if the various competitors have each been disqualified. This must be what Churchill had in mind when he famously quipped that democracy is the worst of political systems—except for all the others. I shall refer to this understanding as *democracy by default*.

The picture sketched to this point has been entirely negative. It is sufficient for exhibiting the undesirability of politburos and censorious ayatollahs, but it does not answer the question, "Why government at all?" If less is more, then must anarchy not be the most? For better or worse, no. "If men were angels," observes Madison in *Federalist 51*, "no government would be necessary." Human nature being what it is, however, temptation to aggress against the rights of others is a constant companion to our endeavors. Some people are weak, and others, downright evil. Force is necessary to counter the threat of force, and that is where the state comes in. This is Locke's insight, and it is seconded by the entire liberal tradition.

We are secured in the enjoyment of our rights by the rule of law. Law and order is what the economists call a public good. This means that its enjoyment by some individuals will spill over to others. Moreover, one individual's possession of the good does not mean there is less to go around for others. Defense against potential foreign aggressors is an example of an even purer public good. The only or most effective way to protect some members of the population against either domestic or foreign rights violators is to extend that protection to all. One implication of publicness in this sense is that we will confront strategic bargaining problems in attempting to secure an adequate quantity through consensual means, such as market transactions. Individuals will be tempted to decline to contribute their own personal resources to its provision because whether or not they will reap the benefits depends mostly on the activities of others and only to a negligible extent on their own. The consequence is a generalized inclination to hold back. This is the notorious *free-riding problem*, and an enormous quantity of ink has been spilled by theorists aiming to ameliorate it through ingenious voluntary or quasi-voluntary means.[2] Without in any wishing to impugn those efforts, I observe that in the liberal tradition, the free-riding problem has mostly been addressed by substituting collective, and thus coercive, choice for private, consensual decision making. Unlike dues-paying membership in a fraternal organization, inclusion in civil society is mandatory.

Once it is conceded that procuring the public good law and

2. For a classic presentation of the free-rider problem, see Mancur Olson, *The Logic of Collective Action* (Cambridge: Harvard University Press, 1965). An ingenious response is offered by David Schmidtz, *The Limits of Government: An Essay on the Public Goods Argument* (Boulder: Westview Press, 1991).

order is a proper task of the state, then it is not a big leap to maintain that other public goods may also permissibly be secured via the state's power to legislate and tax. Although justice and defense are the primary and inescapable functions of the state, its reach appropriately extends, claims Adam Smith, to "erecting and maintaining those publick institutions and those publick works, which though they may be in the highest degree advantageous to a great society are, however, of such a nature that the profit could never repay the expence to any individual or small number of individuals, and which it, therefore, cannot be expected that any individual or small number of individuals should erect or maintain."[3] Although contemporary libertarians vociferously debate whether and how these activities may successfully be weaned away from the bounteous breast of government, it must be conceded that virtually the entire tradition of liberal thought from Locke through Milton Friedman has acknowledged the need for a greater or lesser measure of political provision. This function is a major preoccupation of all existing developed states, democratic or otherwise. However, democratic regimes may be thought to have an advantage over all others with regard to public goods provision in that the citizenry will support those activities that afford them good value for tax money spent and will punish via electoral ostracism those who squander common funds.

However, this understanding of democracy as an efficient generator of public goods has been subjected to an increasingly sophisticated critique in recent years by social scientists bringing the tools of economic analysis to collective choice processes. Their explorations constitute the discipline of *public choice theory*, and its results have not been heartening for democracy

3. Adam Smith, *Wealth of Nations* (Indianapolis: Liberty Classics, 1981), 723.

enthusiasts.[4] Even supposing that some goods must be funded through tax money if we are to have them at all (antimissile defense? epidemic disease control? NASA explorations?), collective provision carries many overt and hidden costs. First, it is of the one-size-fits-all variety. For example, as a taxpayer you "purchase" your pro rata share of national defense, or whatever, even though as a pacifist or Manifest Destiny jingoist you believe that to be too much/too little. Second, not all votes and voices are equal in determining what shall be procured. Concentrated special interests enjoy notoriously better access to the ears of politicians than does the general public. Thus, third, allocations often amount to blatant transfers from one segment of the population to another rather than, in any meaningful sense, to service of a common good. Fourth, mutual back-scratching and logrolling generate total budgets higher than any of the individual parties might wish. Fifth, even arguably worthwhile public works will typically be delivered at inflated prices because incentives to minimize economic costs are less powerful than incentives to maximize political gains. That isn't to say that democracies do a poor job of supplying public goods; the crucial question is "Compared with what?" Our own siphoners of funds from the common fisc begin to look rather benign when compared with, say, Zaire's late megakleptocrat Mobuto or Argentina's Juan Perón. Nonetheless, it is a clear implication of public choice theory that democratic determinations fall short of market provision in terms of both efficacy and equity.

Public choice theory affords us the most realistic understanding we have yet achieved concerning the inner workings of default democracy. Yet, in at least three respects, it is deficient.

4. The *Ur*-text of public choice theory is James Buchanan and Gordon Tullock, *The Calculus of Consent* (Ann Arbor: University of Michigan Press, 1962). A useful survey of the field is offered by Dennis Mueller, *Public Choice II* (Cambridge: Cambridge University Press, 1989).

First, it fails to explain why what is essentially an economic activity (in which votes substitute for dollars) should be surrounded by a rhetoric of public-spiritedness. Politicians invest a great deal of time and financial resources in projecting images of personal virtue and concern for the general well-being. Even if offered only as camouflage for acts of private predation, under a conception of politics as entirely self-serving, how could these displays fool anyone? Second, why should rational economic actors bother to secure political information and haul themselves off to the polls every couple years? One vote among millions of others is, for all practical purposes, invisible; a person is more likely to be hit by a bus on the way to the ballot box than to tip the balance once he gets there. Because economic man won't bestir himself to vote but tens of millions of our compatriots do, the purely economic theory seems to defeat itself.[5] Third, if democratic determinations are merely a less perfect analog of buying and selling on the market, it is impossible to explain how democracy could have assumed the status of an icon, indeed, the most luminous social ideal of our time. Surely there must be more to democratic enthusiasm than this.

2. DYNAMIC DEMOCRACY

For Locke and his successors, the value of democratic procedures is instrumental: They are the best (or least bad) means for achieving ends such as civil peace, respect for rights, and a measure of commodious living. Running alongside the Lockean tradition, however, is an understanding of democratic activity not as merely the distasteful medicine one must swallow in order

---

5. These dilemmas of *rational ignorance* and *rational abstention* are introduced to the literature by Anthony Downs, *An Economic Theory of Democracy* (New York: Harper & Row, 1957). Public choice theory has returned to them again and again, typically with little success.

to secure the health of the body politic but rather as intrinsically valuable. The antecedents of this belief in the value of political activity extend back to Aristotle, to whom engagement in affairs of state was, after the philosophical life, the most elevated calling to which one could aspire. The concept finds its preeminent modern expression in the works of Rousseau.

Whether Rousseau is to be located within the liberal tradition is a question much labored by political theorists. Here, though, it is enough to observe that there are powerful forces in his work pulling him toward as well as away from the successors of Locke. In the opening chapter of *The Social Contract*, he announces the paradox, "Man is born free and is everywhere in chains." The fundamental problem of social design then becomes how individuals may be forged into a political community while they simultaneously reclaim some measure of the autonomy of primordial freedom.

At first blush, the puzzle seems insoluble. Politics is the realm of authority, of imperatives, and subjects are not allowed to simply opt out of dictates they happen to find disagreeable. The state pronounces, and those who neither flee nor fight must obey. Even were the state's prescriptions to be devised by exceptionally benevolent and enlightened social engineers, there would nonetheless be a morally fundamental split between rulers and the ruled. However content the latter may be with their lot, they are not self-determining agents but rather beings who are acted upon by others who thus possess the status of superiors. It seems, then, that we confront a dilemma: either the anarchy of each man doing that which is right in his own eyes (decried in Judges 21:25) or the servitude of subjects to their kings.

Democracy suggests itself as the way out. If sovereignty is vested in the people as a whole, then all can equally be ruled and ruler. To borrow a formulation from Lincoln, it is the unique solution to the problem of constructing governance of the people that is by the people (and thus likely to be for the people). Alas, the formulation conceals a fatal ambiguity: the people who do the governing may not be the same people who are governed. A vote is taken on the question of which candidate is to be elected to office or which policy is adopted; some vote for A, and some, for B. If the votes for A are more numerous than the votes for B, then the people who voted for A get their way and those who voted for B bear the consequences. It is true that everyone gets to vote and that, in theory, all the votes are counted equally ("in theory" because events such as Florida 2000 are a useful reminder that civics textbooks offer a less-than-accurate depiction of reality outside the classroom). Majority rule may constitute a fair decision-making procedure (although, again, the relevant question is "Compared with what?"), and it may even possess various utility-enhancing properties that burnish its efficiency credentials, but it is not self-government; it does not address the issue of man everywhere being in chains.

In fact, the difficulty is considerably worse than stated above. As public choice reminds us, votes in general elections are only one ingredient in the recipe of democratic politics. Among the other key ingredients are money, information, access to and influence in the corridors of power, communicative skills, and disposable time. These are far from equally distributed, and nostrums such as campaign financing reforms are superficial palliatives at best. (They may amount instead to the substitution of one sort of power inequality for another, perhaps greater, inequality along another salient dimension.) The upshot is that tyranny of the majority over the minority is not the only variety of domination to be feared in the practice of democracy; there is also the tyranny exercised by well-entrenched minorities over unorganized majorities. Nor is this phenomenon a sometimes thing. As the scope and magnitude of governmental activities expand so as to impinge significantly on virtually all aspects of economic life (and beyond), the urgency of investing resources in political influence expands concomitantly. Thus the notoriety of "special interests" as a blight on the political landscape. We should not, however, think of this as an "us versus them" problem. Each of us—unionized workers, the elderly, museum-goers, fans of professional wrestling—is enrolled in our own special interests, and it is no more than an exercise of elementary prudence to utilize available means to advance those interests. One form those means take is skill in navigating political channels. When *we* do so, we are citizens forthrightly standing up for what we believe in; when *they* do so, it is another example of a pressure group illegitimately gaming the system. From a neutral standpoint, it bears an uncomfortable resemblance to Hobbes's war of all against all, albeit by democratic means.

Rousseau was aware that democracy understood as majority rule (let alone minority rule) fails to solve the domination problem. So he offers an alternative conception of democracy that does better. If we bring to the political arena our private interests, then we find ourselves in a zero-sum game of beggar-thy-neighbor. If one acts in the capacity of *citizen*, as someone motivated to discover and advance the common good, instead of with an eye toward private interests, then the game is transformed into a positive-sum cooperative venture. Civic explorations of what constitutes the common good draw on the epistemic resources of all members of the community, such that each individual has an interest in eliciting and respecting whatever information others may possess. And once that common good is discovered, it will serve to unite the motivational energies of citizens rather than dividing them from each other. Requisite for this conception is that when individuals engage in public affairs, they put aside their private wills and act severally as agents of the *general will*.

Rousseau's doctrine of the general will is far from transparent, and one may wonder, justifiably, whether hypostatizing a will that belongs not to anyone in particular but to everyone in general is even so much as coherent. However, if such a faculty does exist (or, perhaps, *can* exist), it will go a long way toward resolving the riddle of rule without domination. By abstracting away from the particularities that individuate persons, it renders feasible legislation that is more than a surrogate for vested interests.[6] And it works against invidiously arbitrary inequalities that grant some individuals much greater influence than others over political outcomes; instead, one's role is proportionate to the quality of one's epistemic inputs. The general will is not only impartial among persons but also superpersonal in the sense of being responsive to the well-being of the community as such. It is important to observe that the common good generally willed is not merely the additive sum of the private interests of the various community members but rather something that transcends their individuality. This is because we are not discrete atoms whizzing in splendid isolation through a social vacuum. We are partners in the social project, comrades, citizens.

This may sound more like magic than political philosophy. What incantation must be voiced in order to silence the discordant clamor of many noisy particular wills and bring forth the majestic tones of the general will? Pious admonitions televised during the two weeks prior to each election that beseech citizens to leave the comforts of their sofas and exercise their

---

6. This is also the aim of Rawls's device of the veil of ignorance enveloping contractors in the original position. See John Rawls, *A Theory of Justice* (Cambridge: Harvard University Press, 1971).

franchise to vote clearly will not suffice. Even if the so-called public service announcements do persuade people to give fifteen minutes of their Tuesday to visiting the polls and pulling a few levers, they do little or nothing to inform voters of the issues at stake or the personal qualities of the candidates. Nor do they tell voters how these political outcomes will affect their lives. Most important, these announcements do not afford one any reason to set aside one's particular desires and instead take on the promptings of a putative general will. What they may do, however, is go some way toward persuading occasional poll visitors that they are indeed politically efficacious. Resting contentedly in such false consciousness, they then will acquiesce to the conduct of business-as-usual by bureaucrats, lobbyists, and political action committees and by officeholders who have been bought and paid for.

Rousseau could not have anticipated the workings of contemporary megademocracies, but he surely would have realized that they are inhospitable to the emergence of a general will. When a few are politically active but the many are predominantly passive, it is inevitable that competition and quest for private advantage will win out over cooperation and reciprocity. Therefore, a polity conducive to freedom will demand of individuals that they take ongoing roles in political decision making. Contemporary disciples of Rousseau travel under different guises,[7]

7. *Deliberative democracy* emphasizes the status of the political arena as a forum for free and unconstrained discussion and debate. Its guiding spirit is Jurgen Habermas. A representative selection of his writings can be found in Steven Seidman, ed., *Habermas on Society and Politics: A Reader* (Boston: Beacon Press, 1989). See also his contribution to James Bohman and William Rehg, eds., *Deliberative Democracy: Essays on Reason and Politics* (Cambridge: MIT Press, 1997). Another strand of the Rousseau lineage is *civic republicanism*. See Philip Pettit, *Republicanism: A Theory of Freedom and Government* (Oxford: Oxford University Press, 1997). Rousseau himself shows the influence of renaissance republicanism, and so there is some symmetry in contemporary republicanism taking its bearings in part from Rousseau. Benjamin

but they all agree that full citizenship extends far beyond exercising the franchise. It additionally includes self-education, participation in deliberative assemblies, willingness to occupy offices and assume other political roles, and so on. Politics so understood is not the full-time occupation of some and an occasional diversion from one's real business for the many; it is a primary concern for everyone. Those who are otherwise inclined will be encouraged, gently or otherwise, to shift their priorities. At the extreme, they must be forced to be free.

I shall refer to variations on this understanding as *dynamic democracy*. Unlike democracy by default, its legitimation does not rest on being the lesser evil, nor is it appraised in terms of instrumental efficacy in providing public goods. Rather, dynamic democracy presents itself as transformative. It takes private individuals and turns them into citizens. Advertisements in the media address their pitches to us as consumers of private goods, but cooperative political activity in a democracy is the business of people who take themselves to be productive partners in a public enterprise in which the good of each is subsumed under the good of all. It is dynamic because it points beyond our passive acquiescence to whatever appetites we may happen to possess at the moment. We find ourselves directed toward ends that transcend the narrow contours of the self. We learn to ask not "What's in it for me?" but "How may we live well together?"

Such is the theory, and, of course, it admits of grander and more modest forms. This is not the venue for mapping out

---

Barber espouses what he dubs *strong democracy*, an especially ambitious version of participatory democracy that displays no little contempt for the pallid political forms of existing liberal democracies. See his *A Place for Us: How to Make Society Civil and Democracy Strong* (New York: Hill and Wang, 1998) and the pieces collected in Barber, ed., *A Passion for Democracy: American Essays* (Princeton: Princeton University Press, 1998).

subdivisions of dynamic democracy, but even the cursory over-view presented above should serve to indicate wherein lies its potent appeal. Dynamic democracy incorporates many of the aspects of human relationships we most prize: rational dis-course, cooperative interchange, friendship among equals, en-rollment in an enterprise that transcends the individual. Politics so understood is not merely a mechanism for the provision of goods and services when market failures render ordinary eco-nomic transactions unwieldy; it is a mode of association valuable in its own right. Enthusiasts see dynamic democracy as an al-ternative to fierce corporate competition and bureaucracy's deadening monotony. Buyers and sellers, employers and em-ployees, rich and poor are pulled apart by conflicting private interests; citizens, though, are drawn together under conditions of democratic equality.

The ideal possesses general appeal, but it is especially attrac-tive to those who have recently emerged from totalitarian re-gimes or to those who, like the students jamming Tiananmen Square, aspire to do so. Where the chains of political domina-tion are especially prominent, release is most eagerly sought. In such political environments, one's neighbor or coworker or kinsman may seem to be a friend but may instead be a Stasi informant. Suspicion is an everyday fact of life, and fellowship is thereby imperiled. The desire for democracy is a desire to overcome alienation of each from the rest. It is not surprising, then, that in the aftermath of the century of the great despot-isms, democracy is the single most luminous ideal of those seeking to regain the freedom into which, on the authority of Rousseau, they were born.

So much for luminous ideals; inconvenient realities must now have their turn. The gap between dynamic democracy's ideals and real-world democratic practice is wide. Overcoming it will require truly heroic measures, if indeed it can be overcome.

First, downsizing and otherwise restructuring political institutions will almost certainly be necessary. Town meetings and the intense civil life of small republics are not transplantable in any obvious manner into the modern state that counts its population in the tens or hundreds of millions. The latter requires full-time specialists tending to operations, not merely the voluntary contributions of citizen-generalists. For this reason, Rousseau himself surely would demand the dismantling of megapolities into smaller, more intimate associations. The ideal of dynamic democracy is, thus, utopian. But second, it is also starkly dystopian, for it demands not only social engineering but also vigorous human engineering. People whose preferences run to involvement in markets or family or small-scale association will have to be reeducated so that they will instead come to prefer taking up roles within the wider polity. And make no mistake about it: These roles will make extensive demands on people's time and energies, and the required reeducation will be similarly extensive. Is this freedom? Certainly not in the ordinary sense of leaving people alone to follow their own conception of the good life. Rather, it bears an uncomfortably close resemblance to the freedom from iniquity that zealous inquisitors have offered to less-than-willing buyers throughout the ages. Not surprisingly, the inquisitors always seem to enjoy a great deal more garden-variety freedom than do their reluctant pupils. One need not be an inveterate cynic to suspect that the most ardent proponents of dynamic democracy anticipate a vast heightening of their own political status under the system they recommend. Inequalities take various forms, and rule by the self-proclaimed wise is not necessarily one of the most benign.

Although there is much more to be said on these matters, the foregoing is sufficient to suggest that democrats confront something of a paradox: A democracy that is reasonably efficient and constrained is too lackluster to address deep moral concerns, but a democracy responsive to ideals of fellowship and self-transfiguration is incipiently totalitarian and of dubious practicality. Might there nonetheless be some way to square the circle? The next section broaches a resolution.

3. EXPRESSIVE DEMOCRACY[8]

There are several reasons to believe that the neat schematism of the preceding two sections is too neat. First, although it locates democratic passions entirely on the side of dynamic democracy, significant reservoirs of moral capital can be observed in the theory and practice of democracy by default. Many citizens regard exercise of the franchise as fulfillment of a sacred civic duty; immigration often is valued not solely as an avenue to a higher standard of living but also as the opportunity to attain the status of being a participating member in a democracy. Second, practicing politicians routinely provide a rhetoric the moral dimensions of which are prominent. This practice would not be self-sustaining were it not the case that there are willing customers for this sort of talk. Third, it is apparent that many of the issues around which election campaigns are waged go beyond the bottom line concerns of the voter-consumer. Rather, they incorporate moral dicta that make no obvious plea to personal self-interest. Fourth, the very fact that individuals by the millions haul themselves off to the polls (and, to a lesser but still appreciable extent, educate themselves concerning issues and candidates) despite the lack of any direct benefit to themselves in casting a ballot that almost certainly will have no effect on who wins and who loses is presumptive evidence that

8. The model of expressive voting offered in this section is developed more fully in Geoffrey Brennan and Loren Lomasky, *Democracy and Decision: The Pure Theory of Electoral Preference* (New York: Cambridge University Press, 1993).

their actions are motivated by something other than narrow material interest.

As noted in section 1, orthodox public choice theory has an extraordinarily difficult time explaining these circumstances of democratic involvement. It attempts to explain away the moral rhetoric surrounding elections as no more than epiphenomenal camouflage and trips to the polls as resulting from some combination of ignorance and extreme risk aversion on the part of voters. These theoretical animadversions are patently ad hoc devices to preserve the hypothesis that *homo economicus* does not undergo a radical personality shift when donning the mask of *homo politicus*. But despite their inherent implausibility, the basic instincts of public choice theory are sound. The pursuit of self-interest that explains people's behavior in the marketplace cannot, except at the prohibitive cost of theoretical schizophrenia, be set aside when trying to understand people's performances at the polls. Integration of the self is nonnegotiable.

In small, close-knit groups it may realistically be believed that one's individual voice and vote will have some appreciable likelihood of influencing political outcomes. So from the perspective of prudence, it makes sense to invest an appreciable quantity of one's resources in "having a say" and ensuring that it is heard. One's voice and vote are *consequential*. However, in large-number electorates, there is a vanishingly small probability that an individual's vote (or voice) will swing an election. In the aftermath of the 2000 presidential contest, pundits solemnly intoned over and over again that the one thing this election proved is that every vote matters. It proved no such thing. Rather, it demonstrated something close to the opposite—that even in circumstances so extraordinary that they cannot be expected to recur so often as once a century, the outcome would not have been altered in any significant respect if one or, indeed, any dozen Florida voters had decided instead of voting to work

on their short-iron game. (Acknowledging the inconsequentiality of an individual voter is compatible with granting that one
secretary of state or judge can profoundly affect outcomes.)
Palatable or not, the indicated conclusion is that for citizens of
large-scale democracies, voting is *inconsequential*.

It does not follow that electoral participation is either irrational or bereft of moral content. Acting instrumentally to bring
about some favored consequence is one species of rational activity, but so, too, is *expressive* behavior. One who invests lung-
power in cheering a favorite team is not thereby acting irra-
tionally even if one realizes that the likelihood of the cheer to
tip the outcome of the contest is nil. Neither is it irrational to
mourn lost causes, applaud excellence, denounce injustices, join
with others in expressing hope for a better world—all quite
independent of causal expectations. Moreover, that for which
one chooses to express regard or disdain is at least as indicative
of who one is and what one stands for as any buying and selling
one does in the market. For one who holds dear some value, it
is the omission of expressive support for it that would constitute
irrationality.

Suppose that the ethical or religious doctrines to which one
subscribes maintain that those who are well-off ought to provide
assistance to the poor. One may sincerely maintain this dictum
yet provide but a negligible amount of relief for the poor. That
is because to do so is costly. If one expresses support for this
moral principle by donating a hundred dollars to a poor person,
the cost is a hundred dollars worth of consumption forgone. If
one assigns some positive value to relief for the poor but assigns
a higher value to consumption opportunities, then the donation
is not made. However, if it were possible to secure an equivalent
expressive result at the cost of a few pennies, then a greater
incidence of support for the poor would likely be observed.

One way in which the cost can be lowered is via substituting talk for philanthropic donations. Sweet-sounding pleasantries come easily to the lips, and although they buy no groceries for the hungry, they do go some way toward meeting individuals' demand for expressive returns. As the common adage has it, "Talk is cheap." Because that is so, rational individuals may talk a more virtuous game than they play.

Like talk, votes are cheap. The expected cost to a voter who votes in favor of being taxed $100 to provide poor relief is not $100 of consumption forgone. Rather, it is a function of the probability that one's vote will swing the election. As electorates increase in size, that probability approaches zero. So, too, does the expected cost of a vote in favor. In practical terms, all that one forgoes is the chance to cast an inconsequential nay vote. What one secures, however, is a valued expressive performance. Moreover, one does so in a forum cloaked with civic solemnity, one in which significant political outcomes do indeed emerge even though no individual is situated so as to be able to affect these results. I am not claiming that everyone has reason to vote. But for those who place a premium on expressive activity and for whom affairs of state are laden with moral significance, the decision to cast a ballot is as rational as attendance at the big game is for the committed fan. The same can be said about episodes of gathering political information, debating across bar stools, celebrating victories, and lamenting losses. We need no far-fetched hypotheses to explain why millions of individuals march to the polls on the second Tuesday of even-numbered Novembers—or why during the same month millions of others show up at football stadiums. Both groups do so because they have expressive interests in the contest up for grabs.

Public choice theory maintains that individuals bring to their political activity the same motivational structure that informs their market activity. Nothing said above should be taken as rejecting that assertion. The error of orthodox public choice analysis is its failure to attend with sufficient seriousness to differences in institutional structures. Virtually all individuals are characterized by both expressive and consequential interests. In market transactions, the latter tend to dominate because participants generally bear the full costs of their activities. However, in political arenas these costs are mostly externalized. Votes may matter a great deal with regard to one's material prospects, but the essential point is that these are *all* votes, with one's own ballot a tiny fraction of the whole. So one enjoys a much enhanced discretion to give vent to one's expressive interests.

That, though, is to phrase the difference too mildly. In addition, there is an ongoing incentive, all else equal, to welcome the transfer of expressively potent but costly private programs to the political realm. This is not purely theoretical speculation. The history of liberal democratic welfare states bears out the proposition. Functions that formerly were the province of families, mutual aid societies, philanthropic organizations, and economic markets have increasingly been taken on by the state. These include education, provision of health care, disability insurance, old age pensions, relief of indigence, scientific research, funding for the arts, and a great many more. The extent to which such relocations are desirable is a disputed issue to be left for another occasion. That it has occurred, though, and that the magnitude of the transformation has been immense, is beyond debate. Like nearly all great historical shifts, it is, no doubt, a product of numerous causal antecedents, but one that may be especially prominent is the receptivity of democratic citizens to opportunities for economizing on the expression of moral convictions by collectivizing that which formerly was private.

It follows that democracy by default is not the moral wasteland it may at first blush have seemed to be. The inheritors of Rousseau do not have the valuational high ground all to themselves. Even the casual voter who knows little about the candidates and issues is a participant in a morally portentous enterprise. This is not to advance the thoroughly implausible claim that all of those who bestir themselves sufficiently to visit the polls take their activity to be a source of transcendent value. For many, no doubt, it barely registers as a blip on their emotional radar screen. Proponents of dynamic democracy will judge this to be a character deficit, but in a liberal pluralistic society the existence of different degrees of interest in political participation is not prima facie undesirable.[9] Some individuals will entirely fulfill their need for moral affirmation in private, consensual relationships, but many others will choose to expend moral energies in political domains. As with other allocative decisions, choices depend on persons' subjective estimations of the costs to be borne for the benefits secured. These are hardly ascertainable a priori. However, the logic of inconsequentiality itself indicates that among those for whom the demand for purely expressive returns is great, political participation is likely to be perceived as attractive.

Low-cost expression is not, of course, the only way in which interest can be served through political activity. For officeholders, bureaucrats, and other functionaries, politics is a source of pecuniary income. And among those who, unlike ordinary voters, are strategically well situated to influence outcomes, political involvement may in fact represent an optimal outcome-oriented allocation of personal resources. Nor is it out of the question that some voters actually do believe the public service announcements telling them that their vote really matters.

Democratic realities are messy, even messier than the theo-

---

9. That abstention from voting is not morally discreditable is argued in Loren Lomasky and Geoffrey Brennan, "Is There a Duty to Vote?" *Social Philosophy and Policy* 17 (winter 2000): 62–86.

ries that are constructed to explain them. Such complexities should not be allowed to disguise the fact that both theory and practice are to be understood as possessing significant ethical dimensions. Dynamic democracy cannot claim a monopoly on that attribute, nor should public choice theorists withhold it from their models of default democracy.

4. CONCLUSION

This essay has not so much argued for as taken for granted the claim that democracy is the least bad answer to the perplexing task of political organization. It wins by default. Victories are victories, but some are more inspiring than others. To the ideological descendants of Rousseau, this one is insipid. They strongly prefer a politics that wears its moral credentials on its sleeve, one that makes the same demand of citizens that the U.S. Army does of recruits: "Be all that you can be!" Sporadic participation without passion conspicuously fails to meet that demand. So if suasion does not suffice by itself to garner an adequate number of enlistments into the corps of vigorous citizens, dynamic democrats are not averse to instituting a draft. Among some advocates, coercion gives the appearance of being a benefit rather than a cost. But even when described as "encouraging individuals to assume the responsibilities of active citizenry" or, more brazenly, "forcing them to be free," dynamic democracy's endemic coercivity is ill-concealed. Thus, it is unacceptable to robustly liberal democrats. This, too, amounts to a win by default for default democracy.

Negativity can, however, be overdone. It has been argued that orthodox public choice theory errs in stripping all moral content from the practice of democracy. It develops an account of collective choice that is on all fours with the private choices that are made in markets, but it fails to attend carefully enough to differences in institutional structures that render the practice of democracy considerably more conducive to moral expressivity than private choices. A fundamental postulate of economics is that individuals respond to changes in relative prices. Inconsequentiality radically lowers the cost of "taking a stand" in support of one's moral ideals. The act of pulling back the curtain of a voting booth doesn't magically make one more virtuous or less wedded to narrow self-interest, but because one's capacity in that environment to advance material interests diminishes to negligibility, other motives are released. (And the alteration of cost schedules in that environment is precisely the incentive to enter it.) Democracy by default is not, then, a morally free zone. In its inconsequential precincts, moral motivations leap to the fore.

Are we, then, entitled to maintain that democratic activities tend to be "better" than activities that go on in private realms? Such a conclusion is premature for at least five reasons. First, the term "moral" is ambiguous. If I describe your reasons for action as *moral*, I may mean thereby to endorse them, to indicate that they are reasons you ought to hold and act on. Alternatively, I may mean to specify the genus within which these reasons fall but without granting them approval. Perhaps what is meant is that these reasons occupy the same place in your volitional economy that my (endorsed) moral reasons play in mine. Therefore, it does not follow that someone who gives great weight to "moral reasons" in this second sense can be reliably expected to act better than someone who does not. Pol Pot was one of the great monsters of the twentieth (or any) century, but the autogenocide he inflicted on Cambodia is probably best explained as a product of the ideals he cherished. No merely morally blind individual could have stumbled into as many atrocities. Similarly, it is not implausible that market participants who lend nary a thought to any considerations other than their bottom line regularly do more good/less harm than those who burn with a zeal for rectitude. This is one way of interpreting the salutary nature of Adam Smith's Invisible Hand.

Second, the inconsequentiality of ordinary democratic participation both elicits moral expressivity and cheapens it. Acts that generate significant consequences for oneself and others are epistemically rich. One comes to learn whether one has acted well or ill through observation of what one has wrought. Of course, one may ignore or misapply the lessons, but the point is that there is data to be used. However, when action is predominantly expressive, and especially when it occurs in the context of casting a secret ballot, one receives little or no feedback from which one might learn.[10] Nor does one antecedently have much reason to consider whether the moral baggage one brings to the polls happens to be the best one could be carrying. If I am moved by ill-considered prejudices, the ballot they prompt will not engender damaging consequences for me or anyone else. Therefore, I shall be inclined to invest less effort in improving them than I would in attitudes more likely to have a significant effect on outcomes. One wishes to express support for "the right thing," but one's expressive interests are just about as well-served by endorsing through one's vote what one *takes to be right* rather than what really *is right*. Thus, virtually anything that produces a sense of moral self-satisfaction in the voter is grist for the political mills. Does the candidate smile broadly and kiss babies by the score? He does if his campaign manager instructs him that such behavior is liable to increase his vote total. If citizens take these trifles to be potent moral indicators,

10. This is central to the case against the secret ballot set forth by Geoffrey Brennan and Philip Pettit, "Unveiling the Vote," *British Journal of Political Science* 20 (1990): 311–334.

then the quality of society's political expression is similarly tri-fling.

Third, ballots are not fine-grained. Any individual candidate stands for dozens of separate policies, exhibits an indefinite number of virtues and vices. The voter may have moral attitudes concerning each of these but has only one vote to cast for each contested office. The ballot thus has to do multiple duty as a communicative vehicle. If one possesses but a single tool to hammer in nails, open paint cans, drill holes, catch mice, and remove unsightly body hair, then one is liable to perform most of these jobs unsatisfactorily. Much the same is true if one deploys a single ballot to express several moral sentiments.

Fourth, for many tasks, political programs are a substitute for private undertakings. If it is left to state bureaucracies to tend to those in need, then there is less call for family members, philanthropic organizations, and, yes, profit-making concerns to address these needs. If the supplanted activities carried greater moral weight in the lives of those who formerly carried them out than do the politically provided substitutes, then there has been a net loss. Something like a Gresham's law of ethical enterprise may be operative: The less valuable drives out the more valuable.

Fifth, it is a mistake to suppose that moral attitudes alone carry a potential for expressive returns. As noted previously, sports fans derive considerable pleasure from cheering on their favorites. Only by an extraordinary stretching of language can devotion to the New York Yankees be described as a moral attitude. (Their long-standing superiority over the Red Sox is athletic not ethical.) Cheering, it can be supposed, is morally neutral. Malice, though, is invidious. As with moral sentiments, malice is a likely stimulus for expressive activity. One who gives vent to hatreds in face-to-face confrontations with the objects of one's disdain may incur steep costs. If one acts to impose physical harm, the intended target may very well strike back. Verbal insults are likely to elicit retaliation in kind or worse. Even a refusal to do business with members of a disfavored group carries the cost of potentially profitable transactions forgone. Private malice, like private charity, is costly. However, one who instead chooses to "show those rascals a thing or two" by supporting through one's vote policies meant to penalize Blacks or Jews or homosexuals does so in the comfort of anonymity. Risks to oneself have been dramatically lessened. It was suggested in the preceding section that individuals vote more morally than they act in their private capacity. But now we can add the further hypothesis that they also vote more maliciously. To phrase it slightly differently, democratic participation tends to call forth extremes of motivation. When acted upon in private activity, these extremes typically are quite costly, which has a muting effect. However, when morals and malice are cheap, the action taken will be more extreme. And it is by no means clear that the balance will usually tip to the side of the angels rather than to the advantage of whichever devils happen to be lurking.[11]

Perhaps not surprisingly, the upshot of these considerations is bathed in ambivalence. A default democracy is not without moral meaning for the citizens who comprise it. But this meaning can be clouded, confused, and in conflict with other, darker meanings. Does it, then, deserve the endorsement of thoughtful, well-intentioned people? And that question calls forth others: endorsed compared with what and to what degree? Perhaps as the least bad of the available alternatives. But that is where we came in.

11. The point receives further examination in Geoffrey Brennan and Loren Lomasky, "The Impartial Spectator Goes to Washington: Toward a Smithian Model of Electoral Politics," *Economics and Philosophy* 1 (1985): 189–212.

CHAPTER TWO

The First Founding Father: Aristotle on Freedom and Popular Government

Gregory R. Johnson

THE WESTERN TRADITION of political philosophy can be divided into two opposed strands. On the one hand are the defenders of individual freedom and popular government. On the other are those who subordinate individual freedom to collective goals imposed by ruling elites. These two strands of thought can be traced back to the founding documents of the tradition: elitism and collectivism to Plato's *Republic*, individualism and popular government to Aristotle's *Politics*.[1] Thus, if we are to understand the connection of freedom and popular government

I wish to thank Glenn Alexander Magee, Charles M. Sherover, Tibor R. Machan, David Rasmussen, and Martin L. Cowen III for discussing the topic of this paper with me and for their helpful comments and suggestions. The usual disclaimer applies.

1. I accept the arguments of Leo Strauss and his many students, not to mention Plato's explicit statements, that the *Kallipolis* of the *Republic* is meant not as a serious political proposal but as a thought-experiment for illuminating the structure of the soul and for illustrating the ultimate incompatibility of the philosophical life and the political life, that is, the impossibility of a "philosopher king." See Leo Strauss, *The City and Man* (Charlottesville: The University Press of Virginia, 1964), ch. 2. But this does not imply that Plato was a friend of individualism and popular government. Nor does it change the fact that the collectivist strand of the Western philosophical tradition constantly harkens back to the *Republic*.

and defend them persuasively, we must turn first to Aristotle's *Politics*.

To cite Aristotle as the father of individualism and popular government may, at first glance, seem implausible. After all, Aristotle did not think that individual freedom is the highest political value. Indeed, he explicitly advocates using state coercion to morally improve citizens. Nor did he think that democracy is the best form of government. Aristotle shares Plato's elevated conception of the philosophical life as the pursuit of wisdom. Philosophy begins with opinions about the cosmos, the soul, and the good life, then ascends dialectically to the truth. Opinion is the common coin of political life, but truth is rare and precious, the possession of the few. This does not sound consistent with the advocacy of popular government.

Nevertheless, Aristotle's *Politics* offers a number of powerful and persuasive arguments for popular government as a bulwark of individual freedom. Such political theorists as Hannah Arendt, J. G. A. Pocock, Sheldon Wolin, and Mary P. Nichols place Aristotle in a tradition of republicanism that stresses active citizen participation in government.[2] Furthermore, Fred D. Miller Jr. has argued persuasively that Aristotle is the father of

2. See Hannah Arendt, *The Human Condition* (Chicago: University of Chicago Press, 1958), chs. 1–2; J. G. A. Pocock, *The Machiavellian Moment: Florentine Political Thought and the Atlantic Republican Tradition* (Princeton: Princeton University Press, 1975), 550; Sheldon Wolin, *Politics and Vision* (Boston: Little, Brown, 1960), 57–8; Mary P. Nichols, *Citizens and Statesmen: A Study of Aristotle's Politics* (Lanham, Md.: Rowman and Littlefield, 1992). Although Nichols takes seriously Aristotle's case for popular participation, she explicitly differentiates her reading of Aristotle from those of Arendt, Pocock, and Wolin by emphasizing the necessity of statesmanship to guide popular participation. In this, she seeks to incorporate elements of the aristocratic interpretation of Aristotle offered by Strauss (*The City and Man*, ch. 1) and his students: Carnes Lord, "Politics and Philosophy in Aristotle's *Politics*," *Hermes* 106 (1978): 336–57; Delba Winthrop, "Aristotle on Participatory Democracy," *Polity* 11 (1978): 151–71.

the tradition of natural rights theory, one of the richest sources of arguments for individual freedom and popular rule.[3] Finally, both John Adams and Thomas Jefferson saw Aristotle as one of the first formulators of the principles of the American founding, a view seconded by such scholars as Harvey C. Mansfield Jr., Charles M. Sherover, Paul A. Rahe, and Carl J. Richard.[4]

I. THE NECESSITY OF POLITICS

Aristotle is famous for holding that man is by nature a political animal. But what does this mean? Aristotle explains that "even when human beings are not in need of each other's help, they have no less desire to live together, though it is also true that the common advantage draws them into union insofar as noble living is something they each partake of. So this above all is the end, whether for everyone in common or for each singly" (*Politics* 3.6.1278b19–22).[5] Here Aristotle contrasts two different

3. Fred D. Miller Jr., *Nature, Justice, and Rights in Aristotle's Politics* (Oxford: Clarendon Press, 1995). See also *Aristotle's Politics: A Symposium, The Review of Metaphysics* 49, no. 4 (June 1996), which consists of six extensive papers on Miller's book and Miller's reply. Roderick T. Long's contribution, "Aristotle's Conception of Freedom," is an often persuasive attempt to push Aristotle even further in the direction of classical liberalism.

4. Adams and Jefferson are quoted in Paul A. Rahe, *Republics Ancient and Modern*, vol. 3, *Inventions of Prudence: Constituting the American Regime* (Chapel Hill: University of North Carolina Press, 1994), 27, 58–73; Harvey C. Mansfield Jr., *America's Constitutional Soul* (Baltimore: The Johns Hopkins University Press, 1991), chs. 8, 9, and 14; Charles M. Sherover, *Time, Freedom, and the Common Good: An Essay in Public Philosophy* (Albany: State University of New York Press, 1989), ch. 5; Carl J. Richard, *The Founders and the Classics: Greece, Rome, and the American Enlightenment* (Cambridge: Harvard University Press, 1994), esp. ch. 5; cf. John Zvesper, "The American Founders and Classical Political Thought," *History of Political Thought* 10 (1989): 701–18.

5. All quotes from Aristotle are from *The Politics of Aristotle*, trans. and ed. Peter L. Phillips Simpson (Chapel Hill: University of North Carolina Press, 1997). Simpson's edition has two unique features. First, the *Politics* is

needs of the human soul that give rise to different forms of community, one prepolitical, the other political.

The first need is material. On this account, individuals form communities to secure the necessities of life. Because few of us are capable of fulfilling all our needs alone, material self-interest forces us to cooperate, developing our particular talents and trading our products with others. The classical example of such a community is the city of pigs in the second book of Plato's *Republic*.

The second need is spiritual. Even in the absence of material need, human beings will form communities because only through community can we satisfy our spiritual need to live nobly, that is, to achieve *eudaimonia*, "happiness," which Aristotle defines as a life of unimpeded virtuous activity.

Aristotle holds that the forms of association that arise from material needs are prepolitical. These include the family, the master-slave relationship, the village, the market, and alliances for mutual defense. With the exception of the master-slave relationship, the prepolitical realm could be organized on purely libertarian, capitalist principles. Individual rights and private property could allow individuals to associate and disassociate freely by means of persuasion and trade, according to their own determination of their interests.

But in *Politics* 3.9, Aristotle denies that the realm of material needs, whether organized on libertarian or nonlibertarian lines, could ever fully satisfy our spiritual need for happiness: "It is not the case . . . that people come together for the sake of life

---

introduced by a translation of *Nicomachean Ethics* 10.9. Second, Simpson moves books 7 and 8 of the *Politics*, positioning them between the traditional books 3 and 4. I retain the traditional ordering in my citations, indicating Simpson's renumbering in brackets. Unless otherwise noted, all quotes are from the *Politics*. Quotes from the *Nicomachean Ethics* will be indicated with the abbreviation *NE*.

alone, but rather for the sake of living well" (3.9.1280a31) and "the political community must be set down as existing for the sake of noble deeds and not merely for living together" (3.9.1281a2). Aristotle's clearest repudiation of any minimalistic form of liberalism is the following passage:

> Nor do people come together for the sake of an alliance to prevent themselves from being wronged by anyone, nor again for purposes of mutual exchange and mutual utility. Otherwise the Etruscans and Carthaginians and all those who have treaties with each other would be citizens of one city. . . . [But they are not] concerned about what each other's character should be, not even with the aim of preventing anyone subject to the agreements from becoming unjust or acquiring a single depraved habit. They are concerned only that they should not do any wrong to each other. But all those who are concerned about a good state of law concentrate their attention on political virtue and vice, from which it is manifest that the city truly and not verbally so called must make virtue its care. (3.9.1280a34–b7)

Aristotle does not disdain mutual exchange and mutual protection. But he thinks that the state must do more. It must concern itself with the character of the citizen; it must encourage virtue and discourage vice.

But why does Aristotle think that the pursuit of virtue is political at all, much less the defining characteristic of the political? Why does he reject the liberal principle that whether and how individuals pursue virtue is an ineluctably private choice? The ultimate anthropological foundation of Aristotelian political science is man's neoteny. Many animals can fend for themselves as soon as they are born. But man is born radically immature and incapable of living on his own. We need many years of care and education. Nature does not give us the ability to survive, much less flourish. But she gives us the ability to acquire the ability. Skills are acquired abilities to live. Virtue is the acquired ability to live well. The best way to acquire virtue is not through trial and error but through education, which allows us to benefit from the trials and avoid the errors of others. Fortune permitting, if we act virtuously, we will live well.

Liberals often claim that freedom of choice is a necessary condition of virtue. We can receive no moral credit for a virtue that is not freely chosen but is instead forced upon us. Aristotle, however, holds that force is a necessary condition of virtue. Aristotle may have defined man as the rational animal, but unlike the Sophists of his day, he did not think that rational persuasion is sufficient to instill virtue:

> . . . if reasoned words were sufficient by themselves to make us decent, they would, to follow a remark of Theognis, justly carry off many and great rewards, and the thing to do would be to provide them. But, as it is, words seem to have the strength to incite and urge on those of the young who are generous and to get a well-bred character and one truly in love with the noble to be possessed by virtue; but they appear incapable of inciting the many toward becoming gentlemen. For the many naturally obey the rule of fear, not of shame, and shun what is base not because it is ugly but because it is punished. Living by passion as they do, they pursue their own pleasures and whatever will bring these pleasures about . . . ; but of the noble and truly pleasant they do not even have the notion, since they have never tasted it. How could reasoned words reform such people? For it is not possible, or not easy, to replace by reason what has long since become fixed in the character. (*NE* 10.9.1179b4–18)

The defect of reason can, however, be corrected by force: "Reason and teaching by no means prevail in everyone's case; instead, there is need that the hearer's soul, like earth about to nourish the seed, be worked over in its habits beforehand so as to enjoy and hate in a noble way. . . . Passion, as a general rule, does not seem to yield to reason but to force" (*NE* 10.9.1179b23–25). The behavioral substratum of virtue is habit, and habits can be inculcated by force. Aristotle describes law as "reasoned speech that proceeds from prudence and intellect" but yet "has force behind it" (*NE* 10.9.1180a18). Therefore, the compulsion of the appropriate laws is a great aid in acquiring virtue.

At this point, however, one might object that Aristotle has established only a case for parental, not political, force in moral education. Aristotle admits that only in Sparta and a few other cities is there public education in morals, whereas "In most cities these matters are neglected, and each lives as he wishes, giving sacred law, in Cyclops' fashion, to his wife and children" (*NE* 10.9.1180a24–27). Aristotle grants that an education adapted to an individual is better than an education given to a group (*NE* 10.9.1180b7). But this is an argument against the collective reception of education, not the collective provision. He then argues that such an education is best left to experts, not parents. Just as parents have professional doctors care for their childrens' bodies, they should have professional educators care for their souls (*NE* 10.9.1180b14–23). But this does not establish that such professionals should be employees of the state.

Two additional arguments for public education are found in *Politics* 8.1:

> [1] Since the whole city has one end, it is manifest that everyone must also have one and the same education and that taking care of this education must be a common matter. It must not be private in the way that it is now, when everyone takes care of their own children privately and teaches them whatever private learning they think best. Of common things, the training must be common. [2] At the same time, no citizen should even think he belongs to himself but instead that each belongs to the city, for each is part of the city. The care of each part, however, naturally looks to the care of the whole, and to this extent praise might be due to the Spartans, for they devote the most serious attention to their children and do so in common. (8.1[5.1].1337a21–32)

The second argument is both weak and question-begging. Although it may be useful for citizens to think that they belong to the city, not themselves, Aristotle offers no reason to believe that this is true. Furthermore, the citizens would not think so unless they received precisely the collective education that needs to be established. The first argument, however, is quite strong. If the single, overriding aim of political life is the happiness of the citizens and if this aim is best attained by public education, then no regime can be legitimate if it fails to provide public education.[6]

Another argument for public moral education can be constructed from the overall argument of the *Politics*. Because public education is more widely distributed than private education, other things being equal, the populace will become more virtuous on the whole. As we shall see, it is widespread virtue that makes popular government possible. Popular government is, moreover, one of the bulwarks of popular liberty. Compulsory public education in virtue, therefore, is a bulwark of liberty.

2. POLITICS AND FREEDOM

Aristotle's emphasis on compulsory moral education puts him in the "positive" libertarian camp. For Aristotle, a free man is not merely any man who lives in a free society. A free man possesses certain traits of character that allow him to govern himself responsibly and attain happiness. These traits are, however, the product of a long process of compulsory tutelage. But such compulsion can be justified only by the production of a free and happy individual, and its scope is therefore limited by

6. A useful commentary on these and other Aristotelian arguments for public education is Randall R. Curren, *Aristotle on the Necessity of Public Education* (Lanham, Md.: Rowman and Littlefield, 2000).

this goal. Because Aristotle ultimately accepted the Socratic principle that all men desire happiness, education merely compels us to do what we really want. It frees us *from* our own ignorance, folly, and irrationality and frees us *for* our own self-actualization. This may be the rationale for Aristotle's claim that "the law's laying down of what is decent is not oppressive" (*NE* 10.9.1180a24). Because Aristotle thinks that freedom from the internal compulsion of the passions is more important than freedom from the external compulsion of force and that force can quell the passions and establish virtue's empire over them, Aristotle believes as much as Rousseau that we can be forced to be free.

But throughout the *Politics*, Aristotle shows that he is concerned to protect "negative" liberty as well. In *Politics* 2.2–2.5, Aristotle ingeniously defends private families, private property, and private enterprise from Plato's communistic proposals in the *Republic*, thereby preserving the freedom of large spheres of human activity. Aristotle's concern with privacy is evident in his criticism of a proposal of Hippodamus of Miletus that would encourage spies and informers (2.8.1268b22). Aristotle is concerned to create a regime in which the rich do not enslave the poor and the poor do not plunder the rich (3.10.1281a13–27). Second Amendment enthusiasts will be gratified at Aristotle's emphasis on the importance of a wide distribution of arms in maintaining the freedom of the populace (2.8.1268a16–24; 3.17.1288a12–14; 4.3[6.3].1289b27–40; 4.13[6.13].1297a12–27; 7.11[4.11].1330b17–20). War and empire are great enemies of liberty, so isolationists and peace lovers will be gratified by Aristotle's critique of warlike regimes and praise of peace. The good life requires peace and leisure. War is not an end in itself but merely a means to ensure peace (7.14[4.14].1334a2–10; 2.9.1271a41–b9). The best regime is not oriented outward, toward dominating other peoples, but inward, toward the happiness of its own. The best regime is an earthly analogue of the Prime Mover. It is self-sufficient and turned inward upon itself (7.3[4.3].1325a14–31). Granted, Aristotle may not think that negative liberty is the whole of the good life, but it is an important component that needs to be safeguarded.[7]

3. THE ELEMENTS OF POLITICS AND THE MIXED REGIME

Because the aim of political association is the good life, the best political regime is the one that best delivers the good life. Delivering the good life can be broken down into two components: production and distribution. There are two basic kinds of goods: the goods of the body and the goods of the soul.[8] Both sorts of goods can be produced and distributed privately and publicly, but Aristotle treats the production and distribution of bodily goods as primarily private, whereas he treats the production and distribution of spiritual goods as primarily public. The primary goods of the soul are (1) moral and intellectual virtue, which are best produced by public education, and (2) honor, the public recognition of virtue, talent, and service rendered to the city.[9] The principle of distributive justice is defined

7. For a fuller discussion of the value Aristotle puts on liberty, see Roderick T. Long, "Aristotle's Conception of Freedom," 787–802.

8. One could add a third category, instrumental goods, but these goods are instrumental to the intrinsic goods of the body, the soul, or both, and thus could be classified under those headings.

9. As for the highest good of the soul, which is attained by philosophy, Aristotle's flight from Athens near the end of his life shows that he recognized that different political orders can be more or less open to free thought, but I suspect that he was realist enough (and Platonist enough) to recognize that even the best cities are unlikely to positively cultivate true freedom to philosophize. I would wager that Aristotle would be both surprised at the freedom of thought in the United States and receptive to Tocquevillian complaints about the American tendency toward conformism that makes such

as proportionate equality: equally worthy people should be equally happy, and unequally worthy people should be unequally happy, commensurate with their unequal worth (*NE* 5.6–7). The best regime, in short, combines happiness and justice.

But how is the best regime to be organized? Aristotle builds his account from at least three sets of elements.

First, in *Politics* 3.6–7, Aristotle observes that sovereignty can rest either with men or with laws. If with men, then it can rest in one man, few men, or many men. (Aristotle treats it as self-evident that it cannot rest in all men.) The rulers can exercise political power for two different ends: for the common good and for special interests. One pursues the common good by promoting the happiness of all according to justice. Special interests can be broken down into individual or factional interests. A ruler can be blamed for pursuing such goods only if he does so without regard to justice, that is, without a just concern for the happiness of all. When a single man rules for the common good, we have kingship. When he rules for his own good, we have tyranny. When the few rule for the common good, we have aristocracy. When they rule for their factional interest, we have oligarchy. When the many rule for the common good, we have polity. When they rule for their factional interest, we have democracy. These six regimes can exist in pure forms, or they can be mixed together.

Second, Aristotle treats social classes as elemental political distinctions. In *Politics* 3.8, he refines his definitions of oligarchy and democracy, claiming that oligarchy is actually rule by the rich, whether they are few or many, and democracy is rule by the poor, whether they are few or many. Similarly, in *Politics*

---

freedom unthreatening to the reigning climate of opinion. A cynic might argue that if Americans actually made use of their freedom of thought, it would be quickly taken away.

4.11[6.1], Aristotle also defines polity as rule by the middle class. In *Politics* 4.4[6.4], Aristotle argues that the social classes are irreducible political distinctions. One can be a rich, poor, or middle-class juror, legislator, or officeholder. One can be a rich, poor, or middle-class farmer or merchant. But one cannot be both rich and poor at the same time (4.4[6.4].1291b2–13). Class distinctions cannot be eliminated; therefore, they have to be recognized and respected, their disadvantages meliorated and their advantages harnessed for the common good.

Third, in *Politics* 4.14[6.14], Aristotle divides the activities of rulership into three different functions: legislative, judicial, and executive.[10]

Because rulership can be functionally divided, it is possible to create a mixed regime by assigning different functions to different parts of the populace. One could, for example, mix monarchy and elite rule by assigning supreme executive office to one man and the legislative and judicial functions to the few. Or one could divide the legislative function into different houses, assigning one to the few and another to the many. Aristotle suggests giving the few the power to legislate and the many the power to veto legislation. He suggests that officers be elected by the many but nominated from the few. The few should make expenditures, but the many should audit them (2.12.1274a15–21; 3.11.1281b21–33; 4.14[6.14].1298b26–40).

In *Politics* 3.10, Aristotle argues that some sort of mixed regime is preferable because no pure regime is satisfactory: "A difficulty arises as to what should be the controlling part of the city, for is it really either the multitude or the rich or the decent or the best one of all or a tyrant? But all of them appear unsat-

---

10. On the complexities of the executive role in the *Politics*, see Harvey C. Mansfield Jr., *Taming the Prince: The Ambivalence of Modern Executive Power* (Baltimore, Md.: The Johns Hopkins University Press, 1993), chs. 2–3.

isfactory" (3.10.1281a11–13). Democracy is bad because the poor unjustly plunder the substance of the rich; oligarchy is bad because the rich oppress and exploit the poor; tyranny is bad because the tyrant does injustice to everyone (3.10.1281a13–28). Kingship and aristocracy are unsatisfactory because they leave the many without honors and they are schools for snobbery and high-handedness (3.10.1281a28–33; 4.11[6.11]. 1295b13ff). A pure polity might be unsatisfactory because it lacks a trained leadership caste and is therefore liable to make poor decisions (3.11.1281b21–33).

4. CHECKS AND BALANCES, POLITICAL RULE, AND THE RULE OF LAW

Aristotle's mixed regime is the origin of the idea of the separation of powers and checks and balances. It goes hand in hand with a very modern political realism. Aristotle claims that "all regimes that look to the common advantage turn out, according to what is simply just, to be correct ones, while those that look only to the advantage of their rulers are mistaken and are all deviations from the correct regime. For they are despotic, but the city is a community of the free" (3.6.1279a17–21).

It is odd, then, that in *Politics* 4.8–9[6.8–9] Aristotle describes the best regime as a mixture of two defective regimes, oligarchy and democracy—not of two correct regimes, aristocracy and polity. But perhaps Aristotle entertained the possibility of composing a regime that tends to the common good out of classes that pursue their own factional interests.

Perhaps Aristotle thought that the "intention" to pursue the common good can repose not in the minds of individuals but in the institutional logic of the regime itself. This would be an enormous advantage, for it would bring about the common good without having to rely entirely upon men of virtue and good will, who are in far shorter supply than men who pursue their own individual and factional advantages.

Related to the mixed regime with its checks and balances is the notion of *political rule*. Political rule consists of ruling and being ruled in turn:

> . . . there is a sort of rule exercised over those who are similar in birth and free. This rule we call political rule, and the ruler must learn it by being ruled, just as one learns to be a cavalry commander by serving under a cavalry commander. . . . Hence it was nobly said that one cannot rule well without having been ruled. And while virtue in these two cases is different, the good citizen must learn and be able both to be ruled and to rule. This is, in fact, the virtue of the citizen, to know rule over the free from both sides. (3.4.1277b7–15; cf. 1.13.1259b31–34 and 2.2.1261a32–b3)

Aristotle makes it clear that political rule can exist only where the populace consists of men who are free, that is, sufficiently virtuous that they can rule themselves. They must also be economically middle-class, well armed, and warlike. They must, in short, be the sort of men who can participate responsibly in government, who want to participate, and who cannot safely be excluded. A populace that is slavish, vice-ridden, poor, and unarmed can easily be disenfranchised and exploited. If power were entirely in the hands of a free populace, the regime would be a pure polity and political rule would exist entirely between equals. If, however, a free populace were to take part in a mixed regime, then political rule would exist between different parts of the regime. The many and the few would divide power and functions between them. Not only would members of each class take turns performing the different functions allotted to them, but also the classes themselves would rule over others in one respect and be ruled in another. In these circumstances, then, checks and balances are merely one form of political rule.

In *Politics* 3.16, Aristotle connects political rule to the rule of law:

> What is just is that people exercise rule no more than they are subject to it and that therefore they rule by turns. But this is already law, for the arrangement is law. Therefore, it is preferable that law rule rather than any one of the citizens. And even if, to pursue the same argument, it were better that there be some persons exercising rule, their appointment should be as guardians and servants of the laws. For though there must be some offices, that there should be this one person exercising rule is, they say, not just, at least when all are similar. (3.16.1287a15–22)

Aristotle's point is simple. If two men govern by turns, then sovereignty does not ultimately repose in either of them but in the rule that they govern by turns. The same can be said of checks and balances. If the few spend money and the many audit the accounts, then neither group is sovereign, the laws are. If sovereignty reposes in laws, not men, the common good is safe. As Aristotle points out, "anyone who bids the laws to rule seems to bid god and intellect alone to rule, but anyone who bids a human being to rule adds on also the wild beast. For desire is such a beast and spiritedness perverts rulers even when they are the best of men. Hence law is intellect without appetite" (3.16.1287a23–31). The greatest enemy of the common good is private interest. Laws, however, have no private interests. Thus, if our laws are conducive to the common good, we need not depend entirely on the virtue and public-spiritedness of men.

Aristotle would hasten to add, however, that no regime can do without these characteristics entirely, for the laws cannot apply themselves. They must be applied by men, and their application will seldom be better than the men who apply them. Furthermore, even though a regime may function without entirely virtuous citizens, no legitimate regime can be indifferent to the virtue of the citizens, for the whole purpose of political association is to instill the virtues necessary for happiness.

5. THE GOOD MAN AND THE GOOD CITIZEN

Having now surveyed Aristotle's thoughts on the elements and proper aim of politics, we can now examine his arguments for popular government. When I use the phrase "popular government," it should be borne in mind that Aristotle does not advocate a pure polity but a mixed regime with a popular element.

Aristotle's first case for bringing the many into government can be discerned in *Politics* 3.4. Aristotle's question is whether the virtues of the good man and the good citizen are the same. They are not the same, insofar as the virtue of the good citizen is defined relative to the regime and there are many different regimes, whereas the virtue of the good man is defined relative to human nature, which is one. One can therefore be a good citizen but not a good man, and a good man but not a good citizen. History is replete with examples of regimes that punish men for their virtues and reward them for their vices. Aristotle does, however, allow that the good man and the good citizen can be one in a regime in which the virtues required of a good citizen do not differ from the virtues of a good man.

The chief virtue of a good man is prudence. But prudence is not required of citizens insofar as they are ruled. Only obedience is required. Prudence is, however, required of citizens insofar as they rule. Because the best regime best encourages happiness by best cultivating virtue, a regime that allows the many to govern along with the few is better than a regime that excludes them. By including the many in ruling, a popular regime encourages the widest cultivation of prudence and gives the greatest opportunity for its exercise. The best way to bring the many into the regime is through what Aristotle calls political rule: ruling and being ruled in turn, as prescribed by law.

Political rule not only teaches the virtue of prudence to the many, but it also teaches the virtue of being ruled to the few, who must give way in turn to the many. Because the few aspire to rule but not to be ruled, Aristotle argues that they cannot rule without first having been ruled:

> The ruler must learn [political rule] by being ruled, just as one learns to be a cavalry commander by serving under a cavalry commander. . . . Hence it was nobly said that one cannot rule well without having been ruled. And while virtue in these two cases is different, the good citizen must learn and be able both to be ruled and to rule. This is, in fact, the virtue of the citizen, to know rule over the free from both sides. Indeed, the good man, too, possesses both. (3.4.1277b7–16)

Aristotle names justice as a virtue that is learned both in ruling and being ruled. Those born to wealth and power are liable to arrogance and the love of command. By subjecting them to the rule of others, including their social inferiors, they learn to respect their freedom and justly appraise their worth.

6. POTLUCKS, CHIMERAS, JURIES

Aristotle's next case for bringing the many into the regime is found in *Politics* 3.11.[11] Aristotle seeks to rebut the aristocratic argument against popular participation, namely, that the best political decisions are wise ones, but wisdom is found only among the few, not the many. Popular participation, therefore, would inevitably dilute the quality of the political decision mak-

---

11. For useful discussions of the arguments of *Politics* 3.11, see Nichols, *Citizens and Statesmen* (66–71), and Peter L. Phillips Simpson, *A Philosophical Commentary on the Politics of Aristotle* (Chapel Hill: University of North Carolina Press, 1998), 166–71.

ers, increasing the number of foolish decisions. Aristotle accepts the premise that the wise should rule, but he argues that there are circumstances in which the few and the many together are wiser than the few on their own. The aristocratic principle, therefore, demands the participation of the many:

> . . . the many, each of whom is not a serious man, nevertheless could, when they have come together, be better than those few best—not, indeed, individually, but as a whole, just as meals furnished collectively are better than meals furnished at one person's expense. For each of them, though many, could have a part of virtue and prudence, and just as they could, when joined together in a multitude, become one human being with many feet, hands, and senses, so also could they become one in character and thought. That is why the many are better judges of the works of music and the poets, for one of them judges one part and another, another and all of them, the whole. (3.11.1281a42–b10)

At first glance, this argument seems preposterous. History and everyday life are filled with examples of wise individuals opposing foolish collectives. But Aristotle does not claim that the many are *always* wiser than the few, simply that they can be, under certain conditions (3.11.1281b15).

The analogy of the potluck supper is instructive (cf. 3.15.1286a28–30).[12] A potluck supper can be better than one provided by a single person if it offers a greater number and variety of dishes and diffuses costs and labor. But potluck suppers are not always superior—that is the "luck" in it. Potlucks are often imbalanced. On one occasion, there may be too many desserts and no salads. On another, three people may bring chicken and no one may bring beef or pork. The best potluck,

---

12. For more on the potluck supper analogy, see Arlene W. Saxonhouse, *Fear of Diversity: The Birth of Political Science in Ancient Greek Thought* (Chicago: University of Chicago Press, 1992), 222–24.

therefore, is a centrally orchestrated one that mobilizes the resources of many different contributors but ensures a balanced and wholesome meal.

Likewise, the best way to include the many in political decision making is to orchestrate their participation, giving them a delimited role that maximizes their virtues and minimizes their vices. This cannot be accomplished in a purely popular regime, particularly a lawless one, but it can be accomplished in a mixed regime in which the participation of the populace is circumscribed by law and checked by the interests of other elements of the population.

Aristotle's second analogy—which likens the intellectual and moral unity of the many to a man with many feet, hands, and sense organs, that is, a freak of nature—does not exactly assuage doubters. But his point is valid. Although even the best of men may lack a particular virtue, it is unlikely that it will be entirely absent from a large throng. Therefore, the many are potentially as virtuous or even more virtuous than the few if their scattered virtues can be gathered together and put to work. But history records many examples of groups acting less morally than any member on his own. Thus, the potential moral superiority of the many is unlikely to emerge in a lawless democracy. But it could emerge in a lawful mixed regime that actively encourages and employs the virtues of the many while checking their vices. This process can be illustrated by adapting an analogy that Aristotle offers to illustrate another point: A painting of a man can be more beautiful than any real man, for the painter can pick out the best features of individual men and combine them into a beautiful whole (3.11.1281b10–11).

Aristotle illustrates the potential superiority of collective judgment with another questionable assertion that "the many are better judges of the works of music and the poets, for one of them judges one part and another, another and all of them, the whole." Again, this seems preposterous. Good taste, like wisdom, is not widely distributed and is cultivated by the few, not the many. Far more people buy "rap" recordings than classical ones. But Aristotle is not claiming that the many are better judges in all cases. Aristotle is likely referring to Greek dramatic competitions. These competitions were juried by the audience, not a small number of connoisseurs.

A jury trial or competition is a genuine collective decision-making process in which each juror is morally enjoined to pay close attention to the matter at hand and to render an objective judgment.[13] Although each juror has his own partial impression, when jurors deliberate they can add their partial impressions together to arrive at a more complete and adequate account. To the extent that a jury decision must approach unanimity, the jurors will be motivated to examine the issue from all sides and persuade one another to move toward a rationally motivated consensus. A jury decision can, therefore, be more rational, well informed, and objective than an individual one.[14] The market, by contrast, is not a collective decision-making process. It does not require a consumer to compare his preferences to those of others, to persuade others of their validity or defend them from criticism, or to arrive at any sort of consensus. Instead, the market merely registers the collective effects of individual decisions.[15]

13. I wish to thank Martin L. Cowen III for suggesting the model of a jury trial.

14. For a beautiful description of the deliberative process of a jury, see John C. Calhoun, *A Disquisition on Government*, in *Union and Liberty: The Political Philosophy of John C. Calhoun*, ed. Ross M. Lence (Indianapolis: Liberty Fund, 1992), 49–50.

15. Friedrich A. Hayek's classic essay "The Use of Knowledge in Society," in his *Individualism and Economic Order* (Chicago: University of Chicago Press, 1948), argues that the market is superior to central planning because it better mobilizes widely scattered information. The market is, of course,

7. FREEDOM AND STABILITY

Another argument for popular government in *Politics* 3.11 (1281b21–33) is that it is more stable. Aristotle grants the Aristocratic principle that it is not safe for the populace to share in "the greatest offices" because, "on account of their injustice and unwisdom, they would do wrong in some things and go wrong in others." But then he goes on to argue that it would not be safe to exclude the many from rule altogether because a city "that has many in it who lack honor and are poor must of necessity be full of enemies," which would be a source of instability. Instability is, however, inconsistent with the proper aim of politics, for the good life requires peace. The solution is a mixed regime that ensures peace and stability by allowing the many to participate in government but not to occupy the highest offices. In *Politics* 2.9, Aristotle praises the Spartan Ephorate for holding the regime together, "since, as the populace share in the greatest office, it keeps them quiet. . . . For if any regime is going to survive, all the parts of the city must want it both to exist and to remain as it is" (2.9.1270b17–22; cf. Aristotle's discussion of the Carthaginians in 2.9.1272b29–32; see also 4.13[6.13].1297b6).

---

larger than any possible jury and thus will always command more information. However, if one were to compare a market and a jury of the same size, the jury would clearly be a more rational decision-making process, for the market registers decisions based on perspectives that are in principle entirely solipsistic, whereas the jury requires a genuine dialogue that challenges all participants to transcend their partial and subjective perspectives and work toward a rational consensus that is more objective than any individual decision because it more adequately accounts for the phenomena in question than could any individual decision. It is this crucial disanalogy that seems to vitiate attempts to justify the market in terms of Gadamerian, Popperian, or Habermasian models and communicative rationality. For the best statement of this sort of approach, see G. B. Madison, *The Political Economy of Civil Society and Human Rights* (New York: Routledge, 1998), esp. chs. 3–5.

In *Politics* 2.12, Aristotle offers another reason for including the populace in government. Solon gave the populace "the power that was most necessary (electing to office and auditing the accounts), since without it they would have been enslaved and hostile" (2.12.1274a4–6). Here Aristotle makes it clear that he values liberty and that he values popular government because it protects the liberty of the many.

8. EXPERT KNOWLEDGE

In *Politics* 3.11, Aristotle rebuts the argument that the many should not be involved in politics because they are amateurs, that decisions in politics, as in medicine and other fields, should be left to experts. In response to this, Aristotle repeats his argument that the many, taken together, may be better judges than a few experts. He then adds that there are some arts in which the products can be appreciated by people who do not possess the art: "Appreciating a house, for example, does not just belong to the builder; the one who uses it, namely, the household manager, will pass an even better judgment on it. Likewise, the pilot judges the rudder better than the carpenter, and the dinner guest judges the feast better than the chef" (3.11.1282a19–22). If the art of statesmanship is like these, then the best judge of the quality of a statesman is not the few political experts but the many political laymen who are ruled by him. The judgment of the populace should not, therefore, be disdained.

9. RESISTANCE TO CORRUPTION

In *Politics* 3.15, Aristotle argues that popular regimes are more resistant to corruption. Even in a regime in which law ultimately rules, particular circumstances exist that the laws do not anticipate. Where the law cannot decide, men must do so. But this creates an opportunity for corruption. Aristotle argues that such decisions are better made by large bodies deliberating in public:

> What is many is more incorruptible: the multitude, like a greater quantity of water, is harder to ruin than a few. A single person's judgment must necessarily be corrupted when he is overcome by anger or some other such passion, but getting everyone in the other case to become angry and go wrong at the same time takes a lot of doing. Let the multitude in question, however, be the free who are acting in no way against law, except where law is necessarily deficient. (3.15.1286a33–38)

Aristotle's argument that the many may collectively possess fewer vices than the few is merely a mirror image of his earlier collective virtue argument. Here, as elsewhere, Aristotle defends popular government only under delimited circumstances. The populace must be free, not slavish, and they must decide only when the laws cannot.

10. DELEGATION AND DIFFUSION OF POWER

Politics 3.16 is devoted to arguments against total kingship. One of these arguments can be turned into a case for popular government. Aristotle claims that total kingship is unsustainable: "It is not easy for one person to oversee many things, so there will need to be many officials appointed in subordination to him. Consequently, what is the difference between having them there right from the start and having one man in this way appoint them? . . . if a man who is serious is justly ruler because he is better, then two good men are better than one" (3.16.1287b8–12; cf. 3.16.1287b25–29). Because total kingship is unworkable, kings must necessarily appoint superior men as "peers" to help them. But if total kingship must create an aristocracy, then why not have aristocracy from the start? This argument could, however, be pushed further to make a case for popular government. An aristocracy cannot effectively rule the people without the active participation of some and the passive acquiescence of the rest. As we have seen, Aristotle argues that the best way to bring this about is popular government. But if aristocracy must eventually bring the populace into the regime, then why not include them from the very beginning?

II. WHEN REGIMES FAIL

In *Politics* 4.2[6.2], Aristotle returns to his list of pure regime types. The three just regimes are kingship, aristocracy, and polity; the three unjust ones are tyranny, oligarchy, and democracy. Aristotle proceeds to rank the three just regimes in terms of the kinds of virtues they require. He identifies kingship and aristocracy as the best regimes because they are both founded on "fully equipped virtue" (4.2[6.2].1289a31). Of the two, kingship is the very best, for it depends upon a virtue so superlative that it is possessed by only one man. Aristocracy is less exalted because it presupposes somewhat more broadly distributed and therefore less-exalted virtue. Polity depends upon even more widespread and modest virtue. Furthermore, the populace, unlike kings and aristocrats, lacks the full compliment of material equipment necessary to fully exercise such virtues as magnificence.

By this ranking, polity is not the best regime but the least of the good ones. But Aristotle then offers a new, politically realistic standard for ranking the just regimes that reverses their order. Kingship may be the best regime from a morally idealistic perspective, but when it degenerates, it turns into tyranny, which is the worst regime. Aristocracy may be the second-best regime from a morally idealistic perspective, but when it degenerates, it turns into oligarchy, which is the second-worst regime. Polity may be the third choice of the moral idealist, but when it degenerates, it merely becomes democracy, which is the best of a bad lot.

Because degeneration is inevitable, the political realist ranks regimes not only in terms of their best performances, but also in terms of their worst. By this standard, polity is the best of the good regimes and kingship the worst. Kingship is best under ideal conditions, polity under real conditions. Kingship is a sleek Jaguar, polity a dowdy Volvo. On the road, the Jaguar is clearly better. But when they go in the ditch, the Volvo shows itself to be the better car overall.

12. THE MIDDLE-CLASS REGIME

Aristotle displays the same political realism in his praise of the middle-class regime in *Politics* 4.11[6.11]: "If we judge neither by a virtue that is beyond the reach of private individuals, nor by an education requiring a nature and equipment dependent on chance, nor again a regime that is as one would pray for, but by a way of life that most can share in common together and by a regime that most cities can participate in . . . ," then a large, politically enfranchised middle class has much to recommend it: "In the case of political community . . . the one that is based on those in the middle is best, and . . . cities capable of being well governed are those sorts where the middle is large . . . " (4.11[6.11].1295b35–36). Because the middle class is the wealthier stratum of the common people, Aristotle's arguments for middle-class government are ipso facto arguments for popular government. Aristotle makes it clear from the beginning, however, that he is not talking about a purely popular regime but a mixed one compounded out of a middle-class populace and those elements of aristocracy that are not out of the reach of most cities (4.11[6.11].1295a30–34).

Aristotle's first argument for the middle regime seems a sophistry: "If it was nobly said in the *Ethics* that the happy way of life is unimpeded life in accordance with virtue and that virtue is a mean, then necessarily the middle way of life, the life of a mean that everyone can attain, must be best. The same definitions must hold also for the virtue and vice of city and regime, since the regime is a certain way of life of a city" (4.11[6.11].1295a35–40).

In the *Nicomachean Ethics*, Aristotle makes it clear that the fact that virtue can be understood as a mean between two vices, one of excess and the other of defect, does not imply either that virtue is merely an arithmetic mean (*NE* 2.2.1106a26–b8) or that virtue is to be regarded as mediocrity, not as superlative (*NE* 2.2.1107a9–27). Here, however, Aristotle describes the mean not as a superlative but as a mediocrity "that everyone can attain." This conclusion follows only if we presuppose that the morally idealistic doctrine of the *Ethics* has been modified into a moral realism analogous to the political realism of *Politics* 4.2.

Aristotle then claims that in a regime, the mean lies in the middle class: "In all cities there are in fact three parts: those who are exceedingly well-off, those who are exceedingly needy, and the third who are in the middle of these two. So, since it is agreed that the mean and middle is best, then it is manifest that a middling possession also of the goods of fortune must be best of all" (4.11[6.11].1295b1–3). Aristotle is, however, equivocating. He begins by defining the middle class as an *arithmetic* mean between the rich and the poor. He concludes that the middle class is a *moral* mean. But he does not establish that the arithmetic mean corresponds to the moral.

Aristotle does, however, go on to offer reasons for thinking that the social mean corresponds to the moral mean. But the middle class is not necessarily more virtuous because its members have been properly educated but because their social position and class interests lead them to act as if they had been.

First, Aristotle argues that "the middle most easily obeys reason." Those who are "excessively beautiful or strong or well-born or wealthy" find it hard to follow reason because they tend to be "insolent and rather wicked in great things." By contrast, those who are poor and "extremely wretched and weak, and have an exceeding lack of honor" tend to become "villains and too much involved in petty wickedness." The middle class is, however, too humble to breed insolence and too well-off to breed villainy. Because most injustices arise from insolence and villainy, a regime with a strong middle class will be more likely to be just.

Second, Aristotle argues that the middle class is best suited to ruling and being ruled in turn. Those who enjoy an excess of good fortune—strength, wealth, friends, and so forth—love to rule and dislike being ruled. Both of these attitudes are harmful to the city, yet they naturally arise among the wealthy. From an early age, the wealthy are instilled with a "love of ruling and desire to rule, both of which are harmful to cities" (4.11[6.11].1295b12), and "because of the luxury they live in, being ruled is not something they get used to, even at school" (4.11[6.11].1295b13–17). By contrast, poverty breeds vice, servility, and small-mindedness. Thus, the poor are easy to push around, and if they do gain power, they are incapable of exercising it virtuously. Therefore, without a middle class, "a city of slaves and masters arises, not a city of the free, and the first are full of envy while the second are full of contempt." Such a city must be "at the furthest remove from friendship and political community" (4.11[6.11].1295b21–24). The presence of a strong middle class, however, binds the city into a whole, lim-

iting the tendency of the rich to tyranny and the poor to slav-
ishness, creating a "city of the free."

Third, Aristotle argues that middle-class citizens enjoy the
safest and most stable lives, imbuing the regime as a whole with
these characteristics. Those in the middle are, among all citizens, the most likely to survive in times of upheaval, when the
poor starve and the rich become targets. They are sufficiently
content with their lot not to envy the possessions of the rich.
Yet they are not so wealthy that the poor envy them. They
neither plot against the rich nor are plotted against by the poor.

Fourth, a large middle class stabilizes a regime, particularly
if the middle is "stronger than both extremes or, otherwise,
than either one of them. For the middle will tip the balance
when added to either side and prevent the emergence of an
excess at the opposite extremes" (4.11[6.11].1295b36–40).
Without a large and powerful middle class, "either ultimate rule
of the populace arises or unmixed oligarchy does, or, because
of excess on both sides, tyranny" (4.11[6.11].1296a3; cf.
4.12[6.12].1297a6).

Fifth is the related point that regimes with large middle classes are relatively free of faction and therefore more concerned
with the common good. This is because a large middle class
makes it harder to separate everyone into two groups
(4.11[6.11].1296a7–10).

Finally, Aristotle claims that one sign of the superiority of
middle-class regimes is that the best legislators come from the
middle class. As examples, he cites Solon, Lycurgus, and Cha-
rondas (4.11[6.11].1296a18–21).

13. CONCLUSION:
ARISTOTLE'S POLITY AND OUR OWN

If the proper aim of government is to promote the happiness of
the citizens, Aristotle marshals an impressive array of arguments

for giving the people, specifically the middle class, a role in government. These arguments can be grouped under five headings: virtue, rational decision making, freedom, stability, and resistance to corruption.

Popular government both presupposes and encourages widespread virtue among the citizens, and virtue is a necessary condition of happiness. Middle-class citizens are particularly likely to follow practical reason and act justly, for they are corrupted neither by wealth nor by poverty. Popular participation can improve political decision making by mobilizing scattered information and experience, and more informed decisions are more likely to promote happiness. In particular, popular government channels the experiences of those who are actually governed back into the decision-making process.

Popular participation preserves the freedom of the people, who would otherwise be exploited if they had no say in government. By preserving the freedom of the people, popular participation unifies the regime, promoting peace and stability, which, in turn, are conducive to the pursuit of happiness. This is particularly the case with middle-class regimes, for the middle class prevents excessive and destabilizing separation between the extremes of wealth and poverty.

Popular governments are also more resistant to corruption. It is harder to use bribery or trickery in order to corrupt decisions made by many people deliberating together in public than by one person or a few deciding in private. This means that popular regimes are more likely to promote the common good instead of allowing the state to become a tool for the pursuit of one special interest at the expense of another. Furthermore, if a popular regime does become corrupt, it is most likely to become a democracy, which is the least unjust of the bad regimes and the easiest to reform.

All these are good arguments for giving the people a role in government. But not just any people. And not just any role.

First, Aristotle presupposes a small city-state. He did not think that any regime could pursue the common good if it became too large. This is particularly true of a popular regime, for the larger the populace, the less room any particular citizen has for meaningful participation.

Second, he presupposes a populace that is racially and culturally homogeneous. A more diverse population is subject to faction and strife. It will either break up into distinct communities or have to be held together by violence and governed by an elite. A more diverse population also erodes a society's moral consensus, making moral education even more difficult.

Third, political participation will be limited to middle-class and wealthy property-owning males, specifically those who derive their income from the ownership of productive land, not those who are merchants and craftsmen.

Fourth, Aristotle circumscribes the role of the populace by assigning it specific legal roles, such as the election of officers and the auditing of accounts—roles that are checked and balanced by the legal roles of the aristocratic element, such as occupying leadership positions.

If Aristotle is right about the conditions of popular government, then he would probably take a dim view of its prospects in America. First and foremost, Aristotle would deplore America's lack of concern with moral education. Aristotle's disagreement would go beyond the obvious fact that the American founders did not make moral education the central concern of the state. America has neglected to cultivate even the minimal moral virtues required to maintain a liberal regime, virtues such as independence, personal responsibility, and basic civility. Second, Aristotle would predict that multiculturalism and non-White immigration will destroy the cultural preconditions of popular government. Third, Aristotle would reject America's ever-widening franchise—particularly the extension of the vote to women, non–property owners, and cultural aliens—as a sure prescription for lowering the quality of public decision making in the voting booth and the jury room. Fourth, Aristotle would be alarmed by the continuing erosion of the American working and middle classes by competition from foreign workers both inside and outside America's borders. He would deplore America's transformation from an agrarian to an industrial-mercantile civilization and support autarky rather than free trade and global economic integration. Fifth, Aristotle would be alarmed by ongoing attempts to disarm the populace. Sixth, he would condemn America's imperialistic and warlike policies toward other nations. Finally, Aristotle would likely observe that because genuine popular government is difficult with hundreds of thousands of citizens, it will be impossible with hundreds of millions.

In short, if Aristotle were alive today, he would find himself to the right of Patrick J. Buchanan, decrying America's decline from a republic to an empire. Aristotle challenges us to show whether and how liberty and popular government are compatible with feminism, multiculturalism, and globalized capitalism.

To conclude on a more positive note, however, although Aristotle gives reasons to think that the future of popular government in America is unpromising, he also gives reasons for optimism about the long-term prospects of popular government in general, for his defense of popular government is based on a realistic assessment of human nature, not only in its striving for perfection but also in its propensity for failure.

CHAPTER THREE

Thoughts
on
Democracy

John Hospers

No feature of American life strikes a stranger so powerfully as the extraordinary indifference, partly cynicism and partly good nature, with which notorious frauds and notorious corruption in the sphere of politics are viewed by American public opinion. . . . (Yet) in hardly any other country does the best life and energy of the nation flow so habitually apart from politics. . . . It seems a strange paradox that a nation which stands in the very foremost rank in almost all the elements of a great industrial civilization, which teems with energy, intelligence and resource, and which exhibits in many most important fields a level of moral excellence that very few European countries have attained, should permit itself to be governed, and represented among the nations, in the manner I have described. How strange it is, as an Italian statesman once said, that a century which has produced the telegraph and the telephone, and has shown in ten thousand forms such amazing powers of adaptation and invention, should have discovered no more successful methods of governing mankind!
W. E. H. Lecky, *Democracy and Liberty* (1896)

I. CONDITIONS FOR DEMOCRACY

When a decision is mine alone to make, I deliberate, I decide, then I act in accordance with my decision. When others are involved, however, the situation is more complex. When there are two of us and the matter requires both our decisions, the outcome is either unanimous or a tie. When there are three or more of us, one method of achieving an outcome is for us all to vote on the matter. There are other ways of achieving an outcome, such as tossing a coin or one person exerting force on the others to prevent a vote from being taken. But if all the parties are acting voluntarily and whoever gets the most votes wins, the decision has been arrived at democratically.

1. Consent

"Democracy," it is often said, "is government with the consent of the governed." *All* the governed? Must consent be universal? As a rule, we didn't agree on all the motions or on all the candidates; that's why we accept majority rule and don't insist on unanimity.

If twenty of us decide to form a club or fraternity, don't we all first agree on (1) what sort of matters should be put to a vote, then (2) whoever gets the most voters wins? Then democracy is majority rule after democratic procedure has been consented to by all.

Still, few if any political democracies have been formed in that way. Not all Americans agreed to be governed in the way that they are presently governed. Even if 200 years ago a few of our forefathers signed on the dotted line, how does that fact commit us today? Can one person sign a contract on behalf of someone else, to which the second party did not consent or knew nothing about it because he was not yet born? If democracy is defined in terms of universal consent to democratic procedure, it is to be feared that we have then defined democracy out of existence.

"Didn't we all agree just by living there?" Hardly. People

living in dictatorships often desire to leave but are not permitted to do so. And there are many people who would like to leave but cannot do so for economic reasons. In both these cases, continued residence does not imply consent to the government under which you live.

2. *Voluntariness*

Doesn't the consent of the parties have to be voluntary? This question could involve considerable complexity; even legal experts are not agreed on what makes an action voluntary. If someone holds you up at gunpoint or threatens your life or welfare if you refuse, your resulting action can hardly be called voluntary: it is at least to some degree coerced—you might have voted differently but for the coercion exerted upon you.

But coercion is a far cry from influence. You can be influenced, heavily influenced, by what a parent or teacher has taught you and your resulting actions are still voluntary: nobody made you do them, you did them (as we say) of your own free will, with deliberation and weighing of evidence pro and con. It is still *your* decision, however much influenced by others. A voluntary act, wrote G. E. Moore in his *Ethics*, is one you could have avoided doing if you had decided just beforehand to do so.[1]

What if you have been brainwashed? You acted as you chose, but your choices have been severely limited because the media (or your government) have not permitted you to "hear the other side." As a result, you cannot make an informed decision. What if the newspapers and media are all on one side and you never had a chance to learn the true facts of the case? Perhaps you

1. G. E. Moore, "Free Will," in *Ethics* (London: Oxford University Press, 1910).

could have formed a fair or impartial view if you had been permitted, but you weren't permitted. Or perhaps you would have formed one if you had gone to considerable trouble to go to the library, consult specialists, and so on, but you didn't have time or sufficient inclination to do all that. Is your vote then less than voluntary?

We do not have a "functioning democracy," say Benn and Peters,[2] if the channels of communication on which an impartial decision depends are closed to us. Is it then a democracy at all? In the Soviet Union, most people voted, but if they valued their lives, they would not vote against Stalin; and in most dictatorships, only persons friendly to the government are permitted to run for office at all—the choice is among candidates whom the ruling clique has already chosen. These are sometimes called people's democracies, but there is no reason to call them democracies at all. Still, there can be quite a bit of unfairness and prejudice in the media, and it is still called a democracy as long as most adult citizens can vote if they choose to. It is not clear at what point most persons would say, confronted by official pressure to vote a certain way, "This is it—now it is no longer a democracy."

"But democracy is *self-government*, and in a democracy we govern ourselves." However, who is the "we"? Aren't the residents of one nation always governed by others, those in the seat of political power? When Rhodesia was governed by the British, Rhodesians were still governed by others; and when the British left, they were as Zimbabweans, still governed by others, only this time these others were from within the country rather than from outside it. Defining democracy as self-government does not tell us which of these two the speaker has in mind.

2. S. I. Benn and Richard Peters, *Social Principles and the Democratic State* (London: Allen & Unwin, 1955), 342.

3. *Majority versus Plurality*

If there are ten of us and the vote is 5 to 5, there is not a majority but a tie. We are then at a standoff unless we try voting again in the hope that the totals will change. If there are ten of us and the vote is 6 to 4, then of course there is a majority. If the vote is 4-3-3, the 4's have more votes than the others, but there is no majority because no one has more than half the votes. There is, then, a plurality but not a majority, and if democracy is defined in terms of majority vote, this is not (or not yet) a democracy.

In common usage of the word, however, democracy does not require that any person or group have a majority but only a plurality, and whoever gets the most votes wins. If a majority vote is required, there will have to be one or more runoff elections. In the United States, for example, there are no runoff elections for the presidency; some candidates win without having a majority of popular votes. In some elections, however, there are runoff elections until some candidate has a majority.

4. *Frequency of Elections*

In a democracy, there have to be elections. But how often? A nation in which elections were held only once every hundred years would not be called a democracy because the voters' preferences have not been consulted frequently enough. Indeed, some people's minds change almost every day.

Between every day and every century there is a wide gap. The United States has a presidential election every four years; in other nations, there is a new election whenever the parliament sustains a vote of no confidence, which may be five months or five years. There is no clear cutoff point: if thirty years passed with no elections, we would probably no longer say that the nation is still a democracy.

5. *Exclusions*

In every nation, some groups are excluded from voting. Non-citizens may not vote or, in the United States, persons under eighteen years of age. Until after World War I, no women could vote. As a rule, but not always, persons in prisons and mental institutions may not vote. In early America, the franchise was limited to owners of property because it was felt that they had more of a stake in their country. How many groups can be excluded while yet the nation remains a democracy? Again, there is no clear cutoff point—but a nation in which 95 percent of the citizens are not permitted to vote would hardly be called a democracy.

It has also been suggested that some votes should count more than others, though it is not always agreed which these should be. John Stuart Mill suggested that the votes of graduates of universities, who have superior knowledge, should count more than other voters; and the same for "employers of labour, fore-men, labourers in the more skilled trades, bankers, merchants, and manufacturers."[3] Sometimes such plans have come to fruition: for example, an additional vote was given in Belgium to each married man and each widower of at least thirty-five years of age with families. In general, however, such schemes tend to be viewed as antidemocratic.

3. John Stuart Mill, *Representative Government* (1861; reprint, Everyman Library, London: J. M. Dent), 165–171.

6. *"Indirect Democracy"*

In a New England town meeting, every citizen is entitled to vote directly for or against the measures being considered. In ancient Athenian democracy, every citizen—which did not include women and slaves—could vote directly for each measure. But in modern democracies, the sheer number of voters is so great that it is a practical impossibility for every citizen to vote on every measure. Most citizens lack the knowledge and the leisure to vote on the countless matters that may require attention. And so we have what is called an indirect democracy: you do not vote directly for the measure, but you vote for others (such as congressional representatives) who do, and if you disapprove of the way they vote, perhaps you can help to unseat them from office in the next election.

But Washington, D.C., is a long way from the hinterlands, and in most ages of the world's history, no one could have imagined a democracy of such enormous size. It is difficult enough in a small democracy to get a majority to agree on anything. Any "participatory democracy" would seem to be a pipedream unless it was small enough to permit widespread participation. Today, however, "for all the talk about politics in Western democratic regimes, it is hard to find in all the daily activities of bureaucratic administration, judicial legislation, executive leadership, and paltry policy-making anything that resembles citizen engagement in the creation of civic communities and in the forging of public ends. Politics has become what politicians do; what citizens do (when they do anything) is to vote for politicians."[4]

Sometimes neither Congress nor the state legislature, nor

---

4. Benjamin Barber, *Strong Democracy* (Berkeley: University of California Press, 1984), 147–148.

even a city or township government, is up to handling all the details. How shall vast areas of government-owned lands be operated? Shall certain species of flora and fauna be preferred to others or eradicated entirely? Shall certain endangered species receive special protection? Shall wolves be reintroduced into the wilderness to cut down the elk population? Shall a dam be built at a certain place in the river (or elsewhere or not at all), and may a landowner be prevented from siphoning off most of the water from a river that flows through his property, thus preventing farmers downstream from using it? Shall certain areas be designated wetlands to encourage wild fowl to nest there and to prevent the spread of the desert? What measures shall be taken to prevent rivers from flooding? (Levees at one location may increase flooding at another.) Where shall certain roads be built, and along what routes? Must there be legislation to control the placement of every traffic light?

Congress, unable to control these countless details, creates a *regulatory agency*, which has powers to create certain rules, apply them to particular cases, and enforce them. These agencies possess enormous powers, including the power to regulate what you may do on your own land, and they constitute the *bureaucracy* that makes decisions on countless matters affecting the life of every citizen in the country.

What control do you and I have over this huge bureaucracy? Very little. We may vote to unseat the congressman of whose record we disapprove, but we have very little influence on the agency that he helped create. As a rule, the members of such agencies are appointed, not elected, and there may be nothing that your senator can do to change the rules of these agencies or their methods of operation. They are usually independent enough to be indifferent to criticism and letters of complaint; letters of protest have little effect on them because they realize that their tenure of office does not depend on you or even on thousands of other voters. They can afford to thumb their noses at all of us without losing their jobs. When we reach this level of indirectness, there is barely a sliver of democracy left standing, and often there is little difference between a bureaucracy in a so-called democracy and one in a totalitarian dictatorship.

The situation is not very different with the judiciary; a senator may vote for a certain candidate for the Supreme Court; but once he votes for him, neither you nor he has any control over what the candidate does once he is installed. After that, he need not take our views into consideration in making his decisions. In the case of the judiciary, however, this is "part of the plan": it is an avowed purpose of the judiciary not to be swayed by the ups and downs of public opinion. Only at the level of the jury is a certain degree of popular opinion introduced, at least when "jury nullification" is permitted.

Still, for better or for worse, the judiciary is hardly a prime example of "democracy in action." There are those who staunchly believe that members of both state and federal courts should be voted on in popular elections. In our own time, the Supreme Court decides whether abortion is murder, on the grounds of whether one is a human being from conception on or whether abortion represents a woman's freedom of action over her own body. How nine people decide on this has large and fateful implications. Should the Supreme Court settle this, or state courts, or should the matter be left up to the individuals involved? On this point there is far from universal agreement.

2. DEMOCRATIC RULE

One problem that democracies face is that most people are not very careful or wise in their voting habits. The policies they vote for may not be the policies they would have voted for had they had more knowledge or been aware of the probable consequences of their own actions. Here is an example repeatedly encountered in history: A majority of people, seeing that a minority is richer and better off than they are, exclaim "That's unfair!" and vote to levy higher taxes on them, and if they do it one time, they are inclined to do it again: "Take it from them! They have more than they need anyway." The rich, meanwhile, find it less worthwhile to go to the trouble of creating new industries and new jobs because the reward for their efforts is gradually diminished. Just then, however, the voters are becoming accustomed to receiving unearned income through the political process, and when they continue the process, they find that there is very little left for them to confiscate. They vote ever higher taxes to be imposed on the rich, and the rich respond by producing less and not hiring more workers. An intelligent minority of the citizenry anticipated what was coming but were shouted down by the short-sighted majority. As Alexander Tyler wrote in 1770 on the history of ancient Greece, "A democracy cannot exist as a permanent form of government. It can exist only until the voters discover that they can vote themselves largesse from the public treasury, with the result that a democracy always collapses over loose fiscal policy, always followed by dictatorship." Plato fully shared this view, concluding that "democracy will elevate to power anyone who merely calls himself the people's friend."[5]

"The mental picture which enchains the enthusiasts for benevolent democratic government, wrote Sir Henry Maine in 1878,

> is altogether false, and . . . if the mass of mankind were to make an attempt at redividing the common stock of good things, they would resemble, not a number of claimants insisting on the fair

5. Plato, *Republic*, trans. Francis M. Cornford (London: Oxford University Press, 1941), 283.

division of a fund, but a mutinous crew, feasting on a ship's provisions, gorging themselves on the meat and intoxicating themselves with the liquors, but refusing to navigate the vessel to port. . . .

You have only to tempt a portion of the population into temporary idleness by promising them a share in a fictitious hoard lying (as Mill puts it) in an imaginary strong-box which is supposed to contain all human wealth. You have only to take the heart out of those who would willingly labor and save, by taxing them *ad misericordiam* for the most laudable philanthropic objects. For it makes not the smallest difference to the motives of the thrifty and industrious part of mankind whether their fiscal oppressor be an Eastern despot, or a feudal baron, or a democratic legislature, and whether they are taxed for the benefit of a Corporation called Society, or for the advantage of an individual styled King or Lord. . . .[6]

"Highly graduated taxation," wrote Lecky in 1896,

realizes most completely the supreme danger of democracy, creating a state of things in which one class imposes on another burdens which it is not asked to share. The State is lured into vast schemes of extravagance, under the belief that the whole cost will be thrown upon others.

The belief is, no doubt, very fallacious, but it is very natural, and it lends itself most easily to the claptrap of dishonest politicians. Such men will have no difficulty in drawing impressive contrasts between the luxury of the rich and the necessities of the poor, and in persuading ignorant men that there can be no harm in throwing great burdens of exceptional taxation on a few men, who will still remain immeasurably richer than themselves. Yet no truth of political economy is more certain than that a heavy taxation of capital, which starves industry and employment, will fall most severely on the poor. Graduated taxation, if it is excessive or frequently raised, is inevitably largely drawn

6. Sir Henry Maine, *Popular Government* (London: Longmans Green, 1878), 66–69.

from capital. It discourages its accumulation. It produces an insecurity which is fatal to its stability, and it is certain to drive great masses of it to other lands."

Today, however, "democracy has been crowned king. The voice of the multitudes is the ultimate court of appeal."[7]

3. A REPUBLIC

What is needed, it is said, is not a democracy but a republic.

The word "republic" has no precise or unambiguous meaning. If a nation is a republic, it does not have a king or other monarch. It prescribes certain limits on what a majority may enact—the limits are not always the same. And there is usually a written constitution, to act as a guide, so that an observer may know what such a government is committed to. (It doesn't always live up to the constitution, of course.) But this description is still extremely broad: there are many so-called republics in Central and South American countries, for example, which have been repeatedly overturned by revolutions and forcible takeovers.

Plato, in *The Republic*, presented a detailed plan of how a nation should be organized and governed. Every adult, male or female, was to be eligible for rulership; but the vast majority would be weeded out in a long and exacting period of training in various disciplines—mathematics, philosophy, statecraft, and military training; and the small group who survived this ordeal would be prepared at age fifty to be members of the Council of Rulers, holding that position for life. They would embody the highest wisdom in the society.[8]

7. W. E. H. Lecky, *Democracy and Freedom* (London: Longmans Green, 1896), 1:293.
8. Plato, *Republic*, bks. 7–10.

It is doubtful, however, whether many persons today would be prepared to underwrite a system of government in which the citizens have no control as to who would govern them and there was no peaceful way to unseat them. Much closer to democracy, because it provides the opportunity for all qualified citizens to vote, is a constitutional republic, in which the constitution prescribes the rules of the nation's operation.

Whether or not a nation endures and prospers often depends to a considerable extent on what the constitution permits or prohibits and, of course, on whether the constitution is followed in practice. Lecky wrote in 1896:

> It would perhaps be a paradox to say that the government of a country which is so great, so prosperous, and so pacific as the United States, has not been a success; but, on the whole, American democracy appears to me to carry with it at least as much of warning as of encouragement, especially when we remember the singularly favourable circumstances under which the experiment has been tried, and the impossibility of reproducing those conditions at home. There is one point, however, on which all the best observers in America, whether they admire or dislike democracy, seem agreed. It is, that it is absolutely essential to its safe working that there should be a written constitution, securing property and contract, placing serious obstacles in the way of organic changes, restricting the power of majorities, and preventing outbursts of mere temporary discontent and mere casual coalitions from overthrowing the main pillars of the State. In America, such safeguards are largely and skillfully provided, and it is to this fact that America mainly owes her stability.[9]

This stability would have been impossible in an unlimited democracy.

"No one imagines," wrote Rose Wilder Lane,

9. Lecky, *Democracy and Freedom*, 116.

that a majority of passengers should control a plane. No one assumes that by majority vote the patients, nurses, elevator boys and cooks and ambulance drivers and interns and telephone operators and students and scrubwomen in a hospital should control the hospital. Would you ever ride on a train if all the passengers stepped into booths and elected the train crews by majority vote as intelligently as you elect the men whose names appear in the lists before you in a voting booth? Then why is it taken for granted that every person is endowed on his 21st birthday with a God-given right and ability to elect the men who decide questions of political philosophy and international diplomacy? This fantastic belief is no part of the American Revolution. Thomas Paine, Madison, Monroe, Jefferson, Washington, Franklin did not entertain it for a moment. When this belief first affected American government, it broke John Quincy Adams' heart; to him it meant the end of freedom on earth.[10]

After the Constitutional Convention of 1787, when Benjamin Franklin was asked what the convention had wrought, he responded, "A republic, madam, if you can keep it." It was not a democracy they had wrought but a nation "bound down by the chains of the Constitution." John Adams remained fearful that the new nation would degenerate into a democracy. "The people," he wrote, "are not the best keepers of the people's liberties or their own, if you give them all the powers, legislative, executive, and judicial. They would invade the liberties of the minority, sooner than any absolute monarch."[11] If the majority were to control the government, he wrote,

> debts would be abolished first; taxes laid heavy on the rich, and not at all on the others, and at last a downright equal division of everything be demanded and voted. The idle, the vicious, the

10. Rose Wilder Lane, *The Discovery of Freedom* (New York: Arno Press, 1943), 202.
11. Charles Francis Adams, ed., *Works of John Adams*, vol. 6 (Boston: Little, Brown, 1856), 7, 9.

intemperate, would rush into the utmost extravagance and debauchery, sell and spend all their share, and then demand a new division of those who purchased from them. The moment the idea is admitted into society, that property is not as sacred as the laws of God, and that there is not a force of law and public justice to protect it, anarchy and tyranny commence.[12]

Jefferson may not always have been of the same mind on this issue. Having written the Declaration of Independence, he was in Paris at the time of the constitutional convention. When questioned about majority rule, he said, "Educate and inform the whole mass of the people. Enable them to see that it is their interest to preserve peace and order, and they will preserve them. And it requires no very high degree of education to convince them of this. They are the only sure reliance for the preservation of our liberty. After all, it is my principle that the will of the majority should prevail."[13]

Jefferson several times suggested that constitutions should be revised or replaced every generation or so, and others have suggested on his behalf that instead of meaning by "the majority" the majority of those who voted for the Constitution in 1787, he may have meant what is called a continuing majority, including the majority of each generation from that time forward. If that was indeed his meaning, it is questionable whether the inclusion of such an indefinitely large majority would have sufficed to sustain his view that the majority should always be trusted.

The Constitution is, in any case, a strongly antidemocratic document. It consisted not only of what the federal government should do but also of what it should not do. The federal government was not permitted to control the exercise of speech,

---

12. Ibid.
13. Thomas Jefferson, *The Writings of Thomas Jefferson*, vol. 6 (Washington, D.C.: Thomas Jefferson Memorial Association, 1907), 392.

press, and religion (First Amendment); it could not withhold from citizens their means of self-defense (Second Amendment). It could not exact cruel and unusual punishment (such as torture); it could not sentence a defendant without trial by his peers (habeas corpus). It was not the powers of the government over the individual but the powers of the individual that could not be touched by the federal government.

The election of federal officeholders was also quite undemocratic—a fact that comes as a surprise to many of today's students. According to the Constitution, citizens have direct voting power only over the membership of the House of Representatives, the branch of government responsible for the initiation of tax bills and whose members face reelection every two years. Senators were appointed by the state legislatures. Popular election of senators did not occur until the passage of the Seventeenth Amendment in 1913.

Nor was the president elected by popular vote but by a board of electors, the Electoral College. A portion of Article 2 of the Constitution says, "Each state shall appoint, in such manner as the legislatures thereof may direct, a number of electors, equal to the whole numbers of senators and representatives, to which the state may be entitled in the Congress. The Electors shall meet in their respective states, and vote by ballot for two persons. They shall make a list of all the persons voted for, and of the number of votes for each, which list they shall sign and certify, and transmit sealed to the seat of government of the United States, directed to the president of the Senate. The president of the Senate shall, in the presence of the Senate and the House of Representatives, open all the certificates, and the votes shall then be counted. The person having the greatest number of votes shall be the president, if such number be a majority of the whole number of electors appointed."

"Neither the states nor the citizens elected the President," wrote Lane.

His duty within the Republic was only to execute the laws made by Congress. But in world affairs he was the Republic's substitute for a King. So that he might be completely free to do this, the President was not to be elected by (and therefore dependent upon) either citizens or the States. Temporary popular motions or changing public opinion were not to touch him. Local interests were not to be able to bring pressure on him. The President of the United States was to represent no group of Americans, no section of the Union; he represented The Republic. The President represented all Americans. No group had any claim on him.[14]

Today, however, thanks to two constitutional amendments, senators and presidents are elected directly by the voters.

And many a president in a time of crisis, since that freedom was taken away from his high office, must have silently cursed the Amendment that plunges him to the neck in a mob of short-sighted, clamoring men, clutching and pulling at him with a thousand hands. Today that Amendment does not let the captain of this ship of State make one clear decision unhampered by the ignorance and prejudices and fears of all the passengers on all the decks and all the men playing poker in the ship's bar. An ocean liner could not be navigated for a day under such conditions.[15]

Under the Constitution, the federal government could not do anything that it was not specifically empowered to do in the Constitution. The founders were most concerned to protect individuals against the encroaching powers of the federal government, and they took great pains to ensure that there would be only a minimum of intervention by the federal government

14. Lane, *The Discovery of Freedom*, 203.
15. Ibid., 207.

in the lives of the people. The watchword of the federal government was "hands off."

As time went by, however, more and more laws were passed that violated both the letter and the spirit of the Constitution. The Constitution, for example, empowers the federal government to handle interstate commerce and to settle commercial disputes among the states. But the interstate commerce clause is used today to permit all manner of activities not envisaged by the founders—such as "taxing North Dakota farmers to build flood control dams on a dry creek rising in the mountains of Los Angeles County, and discharging into the Pacific Ocean in Los Angeles County."[16] It has been construed to enable Congress to regulate the wages of those who wash the windows of buildings in which any interstate commerce is conducted. It has been construed to permit endless regulations of agriculture, such as the amount and kind of crops that farmers may grow for their own use on their own land (*Wickard v. Filburn*, 317 U.S. 111 [1942]). It was construed to permit the federal government to set the price of natural gas at the wellhead (the Phillips Petroleum case of 1954), thus discouraging the search for new sources of natural gas and encouraging consumers to be wasteful because of the set price. And so on, for countless other judicial interpretations of the interstate commerce clause of the Constitution.

Another phrase in the Constitution that lent itself to extended interpretation was the "general welfare" clause. The intent of the founders was conveyed when a bill was introduced to pay a bounty to fishermen at Cape Cod and a subsidy to certain farmers. James Madison said, "If Congress can employ money indefinitely to the general welfare, they may take the care of

16. Newton Garber, *Of Men and Not of Law* (Greenwich, Conn.: Devin-Adair, 1962), 13.

religion into their own hands; they may appoint teachers in every state, county, and parish, and pay them out of the public treasury; they may take into their own hands the education of children, establishing in like manner schools throughout the Union; they may seek the provision of the poor . . . which would subvert the very foundations, and transmute the very nature of the limited government established by the people of America." When Congress rejected this bill, Jefferson wrote with relief, "This will settle forever the meaning of the phrase 'general welfare,' which, by a mere grammatical quibble, has countenanced the general government in a claim of universal power." Nevertheless, it was far from settled: in today's welfare state, the amount of transfer payments "to promote the general welfare" takes up about half of the federal budget, and the number of people receiving money from the federal government exceeds the number of people who labor to sustain it. Thus has the American nation, while still remaining a republic in its structure, become in large measure an unlimited democracy.

The individuals in any nation who create and sustain its economic well-being are a rather small minority—the creative entrepreneurs, people with new ideas and new inventions, and other people who can put those ideas to practical use by initiating new enterprises and hiring employees. They are the ones who create the jobs and keep the system afloat. But millions of Americans today condemn these individuals simply as "the rich," as if their income had fallen like manna from heaven. They are envious of the success that some have had, and they aim to deprive them of it through legislative action, not realizing that the success of these comparative few has enabled them, the majority, to be gainfully employed and to sustain a standard of living that would be impossible without their achievements. During most of American history, these facts were widely recognized, even by employees who were far worse off economically than most employees are today. Today, however, with endless propaganda from the press and media and immigration from Third World countries where there is little appreciation of the free market, these facts have been largely lost sight of—hence the danger that the entrepreneurial class will be increasingly choked off by the demands of a discontented majority. Today one hesitates to entrust the fate of the economy to the whims of an easily swayed majority, especially when so many millions of citizens and noncitizens are dependent on these government handouts for their existence.

The America that de Tocqueville foresaw in the nineteenth century was

> an immense and tutelary power, which takes upon itself alone to secure their gratification and to watch over their fate. . . . For their happiness such a government willingly labors, but it chooses to be the sole agent and the only arbiter of that happiness; it provides for their security, foresees and supplies their necessities, facilitates their pleasures, manages their principal concerns, directs their industry, regulates the descent of property, and subdivides their inheritances—what remains, but to spare them all the care of thinking and all the trouble of living? . . . The will of man is not shattered, but softened, bent, and guided; men are seldom forced by it to act, but they are constantly restrained from acting; such a power does not destroy, but it prevents existence; it does not tyrannize, but it compresses, enervates, extinguishes, and stupefies a people, till each nation is reduced to nothing better than a flock of timid and industrious animals, of which the government is the shepherd.[17]

17. Alexis de Tocqueville, *Democracy in America*, ed. H. S. Commager (New York: Oxford University Press, 1947), 580.

4. DEMOCRACY AND "THE RIGHTS OF MAN"

If there is no check on majority rule, we have what is called unlimited democracy. Republics typically place a constitutional limit on the measures a majority may enact. But in what ways, and in what directions, should those powers be limited? One answer, which rose to great prominence in the eighteenth century, was "to protect human rights," first stating clearly what these rights are, then enforcing them.

These were no mere "legal rights," the rights that skilled lawyers say you have—for example, you may have a legal right to a "quickie divorce" in Nevada but not in Utah; to know what legal rights you have in the state or nation you live in, you can consult lawyers and law books. What the founders of America believed in, and what was the foundation stone of the republic they created, were moral rights—rights that all people possessed by their nature as human beings (hence "natural rights"), rights that the law ought to honor even if at a given time or place it does not. It is "the rights of man" that constitutes the principal limitation on governments, according to the founders; the foundation-stone of the new republic was the doctrine of individual rights, as set forth in the Bill of Rights, the first ten amendments to the American Constitution. The Bill of Rights provides a partial list of the rights of individuals that the new Constitution was to honor and enforce against those who would violate these rights, and the chief potential violator was the federal government; the new constitution was designed to "keep the federal government in its place" by announcing to the public what it could not do; and the only powers it was to have were those specifically listed in the new Constitution; anything that conflicted with the terms of the Constitution was to be rejected and, it was hoped, would be thrown out by the Supreme Court.

Rights are a nation's trump card in the attack on unlimited democracy.

But all this would have been impossible

> if it were not that an admirable written Constitution, enforced by a powerful and vigilant Supreme Court, had restricted to small limits the possibilities of misgovernment. All the rights that men value the most are placed beyond the reach of a tyrannical majority. Congress is debarred by the Constitution from making any law prohibiting the free exercise of religion, or abridging the freedom of speech and of the press, or the right of assembly, or the right of petition. No person can be deprived of life, liberty, or property without due process of law. All the main articles of what British statesmen would regard as necessary liberties are guaranteed, and property is so fenced in by constitutional provisions that confiscatory legislation becomes almost impossible. No private property can be taken for public use without just compensation, and the Federal Constitution contains an invaluable provision forbidding any State to pass any law impairing the obligation of contracts. The danger of partial or highly graduated taxation voted by the many and falling on the few has been, in a great measure, guarded against by the clauses in the Constitution providing that representatives and direct taxes shall be apportioned among the States according to their population; that no capitation or other direct tax shall be laid unless in proportion to the census, and that all duties, imposes, and excises shall be uniform throughout the United States. The judgment of the Supreme Court condemning the income tax in 1894 brought into clear relief the full force and meaning of these provisions. Neither Congress nor the State legislatures can pass any Bill of attainder or any ex post facto law punishing acts which were not punishable when they were committed.[18]

In the Declaration of Independence, Jefferson spoke of "the right to life, liberty, and the pursuit of happiness." These and

18. Lecky, *Democracy and Freedom*, 99–100.

other formulations of "the rights of man" are extremely vague; it is often far from clear how they would apply in particular cases. Does the right to life apply to all persons under all conditions—should there, for example, be no capital punishment even for murder? Does the right to life apply to animals or only to human beings? May you not kill someone in retaliation for murdering your wife or children? Does the right to pursuit of happiness apply to all persons at all times, even to pursue one's happiness with a life of crime?

Vaguest of all is the right to liberty: liberty to do what? Some would respond that liberty is to do anything besides initiate aggression (use force) against other individuals; but is colliding at high speed with another car part of your liberty even though others die in the accident? There are endless ramifications of all these, usually embodied in the law codes of the various states, specifying the range of punishment for each offense and describing in detail the distinctions among them, such as the differences between murder and manslaughter and the various distinctions within each: murder in the first degree, murder in the second degree, and so on. Actual laws are necessarily more detailed than the vague general principles that state the rights.

The right of freedom of speech and press was of particular importance to the founders, accustomed as they were to having their views censored by various European governments. Governments, they held, had no right to punish people for their views, however repulsive these views might be to those who heard them expressed. Could they express their views on someone else's front yard or auditorium? No, not without permission of the owner: freedom of speech presupposes property rights—you can't do whatever you please on property owned by others. "But doesn't freedom of the press entitle you to place a free ad in someone else's newspaper?" No, not without permission of the owner of the paper; without that permission your claim would be not a right but robbery.

Many applications to particular cases are far from clear. Townspeople claim to have a right to be safe, the duty to provide the safety being the work of the police force. But what if that safety is bought at the price of violating the constitutionally guaranteed right of peaceable assembly? If you have a right to build a new house for yourself on new land, above someone else's house, do not others have a right to prevent you if it can be shown that your building there will cause mud slides on their property below? Apparently, each of these alleged rights will have to be stated in such a way that two people don't each end up having a right to the same thing (incompatibility of alleged rights). Laws requiring drivers' licenses and seatbelts and prohibiting the use of cell phones while driving are often demanded as "rights to be protected," but what if the protection is achieved at too great a cost, such as profiling speeders by race (even if it does make the roads somewhat safer by arresting more motorists who are guilty of speeding)? The neo-Nazis in Skokie, Illinois, claimed the right to hold a parade and demonstrations; but the residents of Skokie, who were mostly survivors of the Holocaust, claimed that the Nazis had no right even to defend their views in the public streets. (A possible alternative would be: permit the parade but double the police force.)

All the rights claimed by the founders are rights of noninterference. Today they are referred to as *negative* rights because their possession by one person involves no positive action on the part of others but only the negative duty of noninterference with their exercise of their right. They are so called in contrast with what are currently called positive rights, which do demand positive action by others. If I have a right to part of your income, then you have a duty to turn it over to me, even against my will.

The exercise of such a right might soon land you in bankruptcy if the amount I claimed as my right was large enough. The exercise of a positive right ("I have a right to your house," "I have a right to an interest-free loan from you with no definite due date") might end your career and would soon cease to motivate you to work for a living at all because your income would be in endless jeopardy.

The founders never thought of rights as including these alleged positive rights: rights had to do not with what you could get for others' labor but with being protected against nonvoluntary interference with your life. The founders' principal target was not other individuals but government itself. The government could not deprive you of the means of defending yourself (Second Amendment). It could not condemn you to prison without a trial (habeas corpus). These various constitutional amendments were all designed to protect individuals against the superior power that governments might use against them.

If your country has been invaded or in some way victimized by the action of other national governments, you have the right to take up arms to repel the aggressors (right of self-defense). But is it permissible for your government to force you to join in this endeavor? By what right are you, an innocent party, being forced to enlist in a cause you may not approve of, perhaps lose your arms and legs, even your life, to shoot or bayonet others to death who have done you no wrong? "Either you believe," wrote Ayn Rand in 1941,

> that each individual man has value, dignity, and certain inalienable rights which cannot be sacrificed for any cause, for any purpose, for any collective, for any number of other men whatsoever . . . or else you believe that a number of men—it doesn't matter what you call it: a collective, a class, a race, or a State—hold all rights, and any individual man can be sacrificed if some

collective good—it doesn't matter what you call it: better distribution of wealth, racial purity, or the Millennium—demands
it. . . . (And) if you are willing to believe that men should be
deprived of all rights for a good cause—you are a Totalitarian.
. . . Stalin and Hitler believe that their causes are good. Stalin
thinks that he is helping the downtrodden, and Hitler thinks
that he is serving his country as a patriot. They are good causes,
both of them, aren't they? Then what creates the horrors of
Russia and of Germany? What is destroying all civilization? Just
this one idea—that to good cause everything can be sacrificed,
that individual men have no rights which must be respected,
that what one person believes to be good can be put over on the
others by force. And if you—in the privacy of your own mind—
believe so strongly in some particular good of yours that you
would be willing to deprive men of all rights for the sake of this
good, then you are as guilty of all the horrors of today as Hitler
and Stalin.[19]

On this issue many persons today agree: murder is a violation
of the victim's right to life. The fact that slavery was not pro-
hibited in the Constitution was a compromise with the South,
and a civil war was deemed necessary to correct that constitutional error. So much was anticipated by the founders themselves, who compromised their principles in order to form a
federal government encompassing both North and South.
There remain, however, some moral issues on which those
sympathetic to Rand's position will nevertheless be torn. One
of them is the problem of involuntary servitude in the armed
forces (the draft). Many contend that it was imperative for the
future of the world that the Nazi and Japanese dictatorships
should be brought down and that this would have to involve
military action on the part of (at least) the United States. The
Axis powers almost won the war before the end of 1942. A

19. Ayn Rand, *The Journals of Ayn Rand* (New York: Dutton, 1997), 349–
350.

response to this double threat would require that a massive military force be ready at the earliest possible moment—five years later would be too late. And so, it was reasoned, a military draft would be needed in order to achieve victory in time to prevent the Axis from controlling most of the world. Thus the dilemma: if I am doing wrong in forcing you (or voting to make others force you) to suffer and die, perhaps to lie frozen in mud-soaked trenches, how am I justified in forcing you to do this even though such actions might be required in order to save the world from a Nazi take-over for the indefinite future? Here is a young man full of promise, with a great career ahead of him, and instead of allowing him to live to fulfill his plans, we order him to learn to fly and to bomb the enemy's cities from the air. "I hereby order you to kill people so that we can continue to live in comfort"—is this to be counted as a heroic battle cry? Have we the right to engage in such acts of coercion, even to realize a goal that would benefit, or even make possible, the continuation of civilized life on this planet?

If for lack of a drafted army our cause had been defeated and a regime of worldwide terror and death had resulted, would we not then regret our delicacy in "tolerating noncooperation" to achieve such a worthwhile end? Wouldn't the victory of the good have been worth achieving at the price of drafting a few thousand men?

But worth it to whom? Those who died before they had a chance to see their cause victorious? To those who enjoyed the fruits of victory while paying no price? Most people, it seems, camouflage the starkness of the choice with consoling euphemisms: achieving victory, serving one's country, seeing it through to the end—which blunt the sharp cutting edge of the issue, sheltering their minds from the real difficulties of the choice.

CHAPTER FOUR

Moral Worth
and the
Worth of Rights

Neera K. Badhwar

> There are only individual people, different individual people, with their own individual lives . . . each with his *own* life to lead . . . each with his own life to *lead*.
> Robert Nozick, *Anarchy, State, and Utopia*

> Utilitarianism does not take seriously the distinction between persons. . . . Each person possesses an inviolability founded on justice that even the welfare of society as a whole cannot override.
> John Rawls, *A Theory of Justice*

> Liberalism is a political theory and politics based on equal respect for all individuals, expressed in a regime of rights, the rule of law, and a commitment to public justification.
> Stephen Macedo, *Liberal Virtues*

THE IDEA OF equal moral worth is at the heart of classical liberalism and its commitment to individual liberty and democracy. This liberalism holds that the state should give equal respect and consideration to all individuals because they all equally share a common humanity that grounds what we call

I would like to thank Chris Swoyer, Andrew Cohen, Chandran Kukathas, and Manyul Im for their many helpful comments, and Tibor Machan for his editorial generosity with deadlines.

human dignity. It is this value of persons that makes them sovereigns of their own lives and gives them an inviolability that no one may override in the name of a higher good. Hence, neither the state nor other individuals may sacrifice anyone to the ends of more virtuous or talented or powerful or more numerous individuals. The moral equality of all individuals to shape their lives as they see fit also entails that the freedom of individuals may not be curtailed without their consent, even for their own sake, by the state or by other individuals. For this would be to deny their sovereignty over their own lives. In short, the idea of moral equality entails that persons are neither mere means to others' ends nor their involuntary wards. It is this status of individuals that modern political and moral thought recognizes in its doctrine of rights and equality under the rule of law.

But what makes us morally equal? *Are* we equal in moral worth—equally valuable? Or is there a natural hierarchy of worth among human beings, as Aristotle and Nietzsche thought—an inequality in the ability to live by one's own reason (Aristotle) or in the will to power that fuels the desire to live (Nietzsche)? My first aim in this essay is to examine the idea of equal worth (section 1). What sort of worth is it, and what is its source? What conception of the self does this idea presuppose, and with what justification? Do experience and psychology support or, at least, not contradict this notion of the self? If they do, we have to jettison the idea that equal individual rights are based on equal worth and look elsewhere for a grounding.

Assuming that the idea of equal worth can be vindicated, my second aim is to see what sort of valuing response it calls for and how respect for rights expresses this response (sections 2 and 3). Rights create a space of protected freedom for us to pursue our ends as we see fit, so long as we do not infringe on the equal right of others to do likewise. More precisely, this space of freedom is protected by what are sometimes called negative rights or rights to liberty, the Lockean rights to "life, health, liberty, or possessions"[1] that Jefferson formulates as the rights to life, liberty, and the pursuit of happiness in the Declaration of Independence. What is the connection between the right to shape one's life as one sees fit and the worth we all supposedly possess?

In section 3, I also briefly address the issue of rights absolutism or rigorism, the view that valuing persons as ends implies that no right may be violated though the heavens fall. I conclude this essay by showing that the conception of persons as having equal moral worth is not a parochial Western construct, as some have claimed, but a conception that has existed in many systems of Asian thought (section 4).

I. EQUAL MORAL WORTH

At first sight, what is obvious is our *inequality*. We live lives of unequal worth, differing both in creative talent and in moral character and, thus, in the good we do, for ourselves and for others. And both everyday experience and psychology suggest that some of these differences may be the result of inherent differences in intellectual or practical rationality or in psychic energy, even as they deny, contrary to Aristotle (and, perhaps, Nietzsche) that these differences exist along race or gender lines. But does the existence of inherent differences in these qualities imply that we must jettison the idea of moral equality that underlies liberty and democracy, the idea that we are all owed the same respect and consideration? Not necessarily. Perhaps all that is required for moral equality are the ability to set

1. John Locke, *Two Treatises of Government*, ed. Peter Laslett, 2d ed. (Cambridge: Cambridge University Press, 1967).

and pursue our own ends in light of some conception of the good compatibly with the ability of others to do likewise and the ability to value these abilities. In other words, all that may be required for equal respect are the abilities for self-direction and for self- and other-regard.

No doubt even these abilities come in degrees, resting as they do on natural intellectual and emotional abilities. Some people may be naturally less capable of self-direction, some may be naturally less capable of objectivity or empathy, and some may lack one or the other entirely owing to serious intellectual or emotional impairment, as in the case of severe retardation or psychopathy. But individuals who possess these abilities to the extent necessary for an independent and harmonious social existence reach a certain baseline and are equal to each other in this respect. They have what Thomas Nagel calls the ability to see themselves as the same person now and in the future, and as one among others equally real, each with his own ends and reasons for action.[2] They have what it takes to be moral agents.

However, it is hard to see how the mere ability for moral agency can make us worthy of respect and consideration, giving us the moral standing that is recognized by the ascription of rights. Surely Aristotle is right to think that by nature we are neither good nor bad, that good and bad characterize only action and character—the second nature we acquire through habituation?[3] And that self-love or self-regard is good only when the self that is loved is itself good?[4] For the mere fact that someone can form a conception of the good life doesn't show that the conception is worth forming. At most, then, it might be argued, the ability for self-direction and self-regard have

2. Thomas Nagel, *The Possibility of Altruism* (Oxford: Clarendon Press, 1970; Princeton: Princeton University Press, 1978).
3. Aristotle, *Nicomachean Ethics* (hereafter *NE*), book 2, 1103a19–26.
4. Ibid., book 9, 1169a11–12.

worth only when the life and self they are used to create has worth. Just as there is no value in a facility with computer languages if we use it simply to create new viruses, so there is no value in the ability to shape our lives if we use it simply to create a new form of low life. But because some people do just that, everyone's ability to shape their lives and have self-worth cannot have worth, much less have equal worth. Similarly, the capacity for other-regard has worth only when it is directed at those who are worth regarding: regard for good con artists doesn't cut it.

One might respond to this objection by granting the premise that the worth of an ability depends upon the way it is exercised, but denying the premise that some lives lack worth and thereby denying the conclusion that the capacity for moral agency can sometimes lack worth. Instead, one might argue, worth of different lives is unique and incommensurable. Loren Lomasky makes a strong case for this thesis by building on the idea that we are the sorts of beings who forge our identities and individuate ourselves by committing ourselves to certain ends and shaping our lives accordingly.[5] In other words, we are *project pursuers*, not *indiscriminate evaluators* pulled this way or that by every passing attraction. Through our pursuit of projects, we *create* value, a personal value that is independent of the moral dimension of our lives. Our projects give us reason to pursue them just because they are ours, and their central importance in ordering our lives and providing us with a personal standard of value rationally obliges as well as motivates us to value the necessary means to them, namely, our ability to pursue projects

5. Loren Lomasky, *Persons, Rights, and the Moral Community* (New York: Oxford University Press, 1987), 31–34. Bernard Williams first introduced this idea in his criticism of utilitarianism in J. J. C. Smart and Williams, *Utilitarianism: For and Against* (New York: Cambridge University Press, 1973).

(58–59). Our projects and our ability to pursue them have agent-relative value—a value for us—even if they have no value for anyone else. If the standard of all value were impersonal, such as the general happiness or the glory of God, the value of an individual life would be measured by its contribution to this impersonal value, regardless of the value the individual herself put on her life. And so an individual's life would have purely instrumental value, and there could be no moral objection to sacrificing an individual with lesser value to save an individual with greater value. What makes us irreplaceable, according to Lomasky, is that our lives have not only impersonal but also personal value and that this personal value is unique and incommensurable. In investing our lives with personal value through project pursuit, we bring a unique value into the world, a value that cannot be compared with the value of other individuals' lives. Hence, there is no interpersonal measure of value in terms of which the personal value of different lives can be compared, ranked, or traded off. Lomasky (1987) continues:

> *A* regards himself as a member of a Kingdom of Ends when he both respects the unique individuality that is his own and recognizes that all other project pursuers are themselves unique individuals, each with his own life to live, and each possessing reason to reject overreaching impositions from others. In a Kingdom of Ends, each project pursuer is accorded moral space within which he can independently attempt to realize a connected and coherent conception of the good life for him. Rights are just this entitlement to moral space. (54)

Rights protect us in our projects of living our own lives, which are no less than the projects of creating our own selves. Rights recognize our unique and irreplaceable worth as beings who create value.

This account of rights as recognizing and protecting the equal worth of persons as project pursuers is a powerful response both to the inegalitarian proponent of a hierarchy of valuable lives and to the utilitarian "socializer" of all ends who fails to see how our commitments to our projects give us special reason to pursue them and how we shape our identities by doing so (34). But even if Lomasky's distinction between personal and moral value is well-taken (and I have reason to doubt that it is), is it true that all lives have personal value and that this value cannot in any respect be compared because there is no interpersonal measure of personal value? Certainly the claim of uniqueness and the absence of an interpersonal measure does not follow from the thesis that impersonal value does not reign supreme. Nor does this claim seem essential to the claim that we are irreplaceable ends in ourselves.

We may start by noting that the personal value of a single life can vary over time. Consider Silas Marner, the eponymous hero of George Eliot's novel. Silas Marner's life as a solitary miser was less worthwhile to him than his life as a loving father to Eppie. But if we can compare the personal value of two stages of his life, we can also compare the personal value of the life he actually led with the value of the life he might have led had he never found Eppie. We can say that if Silas Marner had never found Eppie, if he had lived out his life as a solitary miser, it would have contained less overall personal value than it actually did contain. He might never have known this, of course, not only for the trivial reason that he wouldn't have had a life with Eppie to compare it with but also for the deeper psychological reason that he might never have realized his capacity for a greater value.

Suppose, further, that instead of Silas Marner finding Eppie, another solitary miser with his psychology—call him Midas—had found Eppie. Just as we can compare the possible life of Silas Marner with his actual life, so we can compare it with another imaginary life and come to a similar conclusion: if

Midas had found Eppie and committed himself to her, then Midas's life would have had greater personal value (greater value to him) than Silas Marner's life to Silas Marner. And if we can compare the lives of fictional characters, we can compare the lives of real people. If such comparisons were not possible, there would be no such thing as aspiration or emulation or envy or, for that matter, pity. What explains these evaluations and emotions is that no matter how idiosyncratically personal the value of a life, it is still the value of a *human* life. It is this fact that provides an interpersonal measure of worth even for personal value. Implicitly or explicitly, we use this standard to evaluate our own lives and the lives of others. And the judgments we render are often unequal.

Further, someone who feels like a failure because all he has touched has turned to naught or who dislikes the person he has made of himself and has little confidence in his ability to change may place little or no value on his projects and the life he has created. The effect of oppression or humiliation on an individual's sense of self-worth may be even more corrosive, leading her to believe that she is, at best, a tool of others' ends. Self-regard, too, then, is subject to interpersonal comparisons.

What this shows is that if our value as persons, our moral worth, resides in our ability to shape our lives and to value what we create, but the value of this ability lies in the value of what we create, then the worth of different individuals cannot be equal and cannot ground equal rights and equality before the law. And no matter how pluralistic *is* our conception of personal value, no matter how sensitive this conception is to the diversity of human needs, desires, and dreams, it is hard to deny that some persons' conceptions of the good may be shallow and the shape they give to their lives shoddy. Indeed, some lives may be both shoddy as human lives and valueless to the individuals concerned.

If we can make interpersonal judgments about the personal value of our own and others' lives and identities, then lives and identities cannot be wholly qualitatively unique. In other words, the kind of value created cannot, as Lomasky implies, be wholly unique. But why should this matter? How can qualitative uniqueness be relevant to our status as ends in ourselves? We can see its irrelevance if we imagine the case of spiritual twins, that is, two individuals with essentially the same character, personality, and style of thought and action. This is not just a remote possibility, something that occurs on Twin Earth, but a reality, as studies and stories of identical twins show (including a story, some years ago, of twin sisters who lived together, worked and walked together, and even responded in unison to situations and people.) When they discover each other's existence, should spiritual twins cease to think that they are irreplaceable ends? Should we? It will not do to point out that even spiritual twins will differ in some respects: one might like red wine, the other Classic Coke,® one might like chicken-fried steak, the other filet mignon. For if it is hard to see why uniqueness in important features of our lives and identities is necessary for being irreplaceable, it is even harder to see how uniqueness in trivial details can save this thesis.

It seems, then, that our value as persons, the ground of our human dignity, cannot lie in our scarcity or diversity, like the value of exotic birds. Indeed, as David Velleman points out, if our value as persons resided in the uniqueness of our characteristics, then we would have merely a "market value," a value that would be diminished if our characteristics were duplicated.[6]

We must conclude, then, that our equal moral worth, our status as irreplaceable ends in ourselves, can reside neither in

6. J. David Velleman, "Love As a Moral Emotion," *Ethics* 109, no. 2 (1999): 354.

the personal value of our lives (for all lives are not equally valuable or equally valued by those who lead them, and some may be altogether lacking in value) nor in their qualitative uniqueness (even if, contrary to fact, they were all qualitatively unique). All the same, both the idea of valuable lives and the idea of uniqueness are relevant to the idea of equal, irreplaceable, moral worth.

My proposal is that this worth resides in our capacities for valuing and creating that which is worth valuing and creating, in particular, for creating valuable lives and valuing ourselves and others as numerically unique and irreplaceable creators of value. If, like evil genies, our capacity to give shape to our lives and identities was limited to creating new forms of confusion and deception and harm, we would not have the kind of worth that makes us ends in ourselves, worthy of respect. If, like the cells of a body, we had no capacity to live apart from the "social body," with our own point of view on things, we would not be numerically unique and irreplaceable or capable of making ourselves our own ends.

Unlike evil genies, however, we do have a capacity for creating lives of personal worth—lives that have worth for us as human beings and as the particular individuals we are. And unlike cells in a body, we are distinct and separate individuals, numerically unique, irreplaceable as creators of value, and capable of valuing ourselves as such. The bare fact of our separateness, of our distinctness as creators and valuers, establishes our uniqueness and irreplaceability. The lives of spiritual twins are still two lives and not one, regardless of their qualitative identity. Alpha's valuing of his projects, his concern for his integrity as a person, is not diminished by the thought that there's one more just like him in the world, only separate: it would not be all the same to him if he were killed and replaced with Beta. Nor *would* it be all the same: Alpha's death would leave one less center of valuing consciousness in the world and one less (possible) source of values. He is, and can see himself as, irreplaceable in the straightforward sense that there is only one of him, occupying his particular niche in the world, taking his particular perspective on things, even if his way of seeing them is not unique.

If we are equally worthy, it is because we are all capable of creating value and of valuing ourselves (and others) as distinct and irreplaceable creators of value. These abilities themselves are not *sui generis* but a function of our various intellectual, emotional, and physical abilities. We may misuse the ability to create a worthy life or even fail to exercise it as a result of anomie or despair, just as we may misuse or fail to exercise or value some physical ability. But misuse of or failure to exercise an ability does not imply that it has no value, and so it does not imply that we, as agents and creators, have no value. It is the *possibility* we own for creating worthy lives and caring about things, and most of all about things that are ends in themselves, "in that reflective way which is distinctive of self-conscious creatures like us,"[7] that invests us with value. And it is this that makes us fit objects of "recognition respect" and "recognition self-respect," even when the selves we create fail to merit "appraisal respect" or "appraisal self-respect," and even when we see ourselves as mere tools of others' ends instead of as irreplaceable creators of personal value.[8]

This analysis fits in well with the root idea of the word *respect*,

7. Velleman, "Love As a Moral Emotion," 365.
8. The distinction between "recognition" and "appraisal" respect is from Stephen Darwall, "Two Kinds of Respect," *Ethics* 88 (1977): 36–49. Robin Dillon extends Darwall's distinction to self-respect in "How to Lose Your Self-Respect," *American Philosophical Quarterly* 29 (1992): 125–39.

which is "to look back" or "to look again."[9] In extending recognition-respect to others, we pay them heed, give them proper attention, and acknowledge these capacities underlying their character and personality. And we do the same when we extend recognition respect to ourselves. If we look at ourselves from within our lives, from the inner perspective, and see these powers of creation and appreciation, we can value them even when we cannot value the way we have exercised them or what we have achieved with them. In other words, we can have what Kant calls reverence for the self even when we cannot have the Aristotelian virtue of pride—pride in our virtues. To lack recognition self-respect is to lack an appreciation of our potential for creating value and valuing value and to see our value (if we see it at all) as deriving entirely from the actual exercise of this potential.

It is in the idea of the self defined by these capacities that the ideas of equality and worth, which seemed to pull in opposite directions, can be brought together. The reflective and self-reflective self, with its powers of valuing and creating, has the ability to see itself and others as equally real and equally enduring, extending into the past and reaching into the future. It is this self that is the proper object of respect as well as of love understood as agape, or charity. For agape, the love of humans qua humans, is also directed at all alike, independently of their character, personality, or achievements. Despite the differences between agape and respect, then, they are directed at the same self, the self that Kant identifies as our humanity and Augustine, as the good or God in everyone.

The claim that the object of respect is an enduring capacity for appreciation and creation of value might be challenged on

9. Thomas Hill, "Respect for Persons," *Routledge Encyclopaedia of Philosophy* (online version, 2000).

the grounds that it posits a ghostly self—a reified entity, like Kant's noumenal self or the Christian soul—behind the empirical self constituted by our character and personality traits, a self that we have little reason to believe exists.

However, the capacity for appreciation and creation of value, the capacity for humanity, can be understood in entirely naturalistic terms. The first step in its demystification is to note that saying there is such a capacity is no more than saying there must be some psychological ability that explains how those who create valuable lives are able to do so and how those who fail at first can later change. This is no more (and no less) mysterious than saying that there must be some psychological ability to explain how literate people can read and write and how illiterate people can learn to do so. If there was no underlying capacity to change one's character, then those whose sense of their own or others' worth has been severely damaged—the abused wife, the slave, the predatory gang member, the former Nazi—could never succeed in recovering that sense of worth. But some clearly do, sometimes gradually, sometimes as the result of a transformative experience. A book, a person, a chance event— almost anything can lead to a radically new conception of the world, either by overturning central beliefs and values or by crystallizing inchoate thoughts, emotions, and values into a normative whole.

Another and stronger objection to the idea of a capacity for creation might be that it assumes a radical freedom to overcome the influence of character and situation, and this assumption is contrary to the lessons of science and experience. For science and experience support the conclusion that our choices are determined by a combination of situational factors and character and personality traits that, in turn, are determined by our heredity and environment. A satisfactory account of free choice and agency must, then, be compatibilist.

Whether or not our choices are determined, as this criticism states, it is true that our freedom to shape our lives and identities is not radical, in the sense that we can make and remake ourselves at will. Our capacity for self-creation operates from the beginning within unchosen constraints, and like any natural capacity, it can be undermined or destroyed by accident, disease, or severe abuse. Most relevant for our purposes, this capacity can be undermined by the very identity we create through the exercise—or lack thereof—of this capacity. For reasons that are implicit in the very descriptions, people with weak or unreflective characters will find it hard to change themselves. And people with vicious characters—mass murderers like Osama bin Laden and erstwhile Communist and Nazi leaders—will be prevented by their warped view of the good across a whole range of issues and the pleasure they take in evil from seeing any reason to change. In other words, as we would expect of any psychological capacity or trait, the capacity for valuing and creating value is itself subject to external influences as well as the use we make of it. When viciousness leads to madness, then it may be that this capacity, the capacity that makes us ends in ourselves, has been destroyed. This may be the case with the mother depicted in the recent book *Son of a Grifter*, written by one of her sons, Kent Walker (New York: William Morrow & Co., 2001). At this point, lack of certainty may be the chief justification for continuing to think of them and treat them as ends in themselves (see below).

In this section I have argued that our equal value as persons, the sort of value that makes us worthy of respect, lies not in the incommensurable personal value of our lives and our conceptions of the good but in *the equal worth of a shared capacity*, a capacity for appreciating and creating value. If I am right, it is this conception of persons that underlies the liberal doctrine of rights and equality under the rule of law and the individualist maxim that individuals are free to live their lives as they see fit, so long as they do so compatibly with the like freedom of others. Because the equal worth of persons lies in their shared capacity rather than in the value of the lives they create, rights must be justified as a way of valuing individuals for this capacity, as a way of valuing them as ends in themselves.

But what exactly does it mean to value persons as ends, and how do rights express this value? In the next two sections I will discuss two different understandings of valuing persons as ends and two different conceptions of how rights express this value.

2. RIGHTS AS PROMOTING FREE AGENCY

Rights create a space of protected freedom for individuals to pursue their own ends, their own conception of the good, however mistaken or shallow, so long as they do so compatibly with the like freedom of others. As we have seen, respect for persons is respect for their capacity for valuation and creation or, more simply, their capacity for free agency. Because individuals exercise their agency in setting and pursuing their ends (both self- and other-directed), and they can exercise it only under conditions of freedom, it might be thought that to respect individuals is to want to see their capacity for agency protected and promoted and that rights do just this. But can rights to liberty be justified as protecting and promoting—more briefly, furthering—our capacity for free agency?

We can start with the uncontroversial assumption that it is rational for each individual to value her own agency as a means to, or part of, her own good, and therefore it is rational for her to want a space of protected freedom in which she can exercise her agency by setting and pursuing her own ends. Hence, she needs a principled barrier against being used as a mere means to the ends of others, and so it is rational for her to want to live in a society in which she has an enforceable right to such freedom. But to have a right to a space of protected freedom is not only to have a justified *desire* for such a space but also to have a justified *claim* against the invasion of that space by the state or other individuals. And such a justified claim, otherwise known as a claim-right, implies that it is rational for others to abstain from trespass: claim-rights imply duties.

However, although it is rational for each individual to want others to abstain, what makes it rational for others to abstain? The exercise of agency requires resources, and in a world of separate, private ends and limited resources, there is always a possibility of conflict between different individuals' pursuit of their ends. If rights are justified as principles for furthering the capacity for agency, why shouldn't others use us as mere means to their ends when doing so furthers their own agency? After all, respect for rights is respect not only for others' rights but also one's own. It looks like the "agency furthering" conception of rights quickly leads to a situation in which respect for one's own rights conflicts with respect for others' rights.

It also seems to fail to provide a principled barrier against forcible paternalism. When people act in ways that undermine their agency, by, say, putting themselves in abusive situations or becoming addicted to drugs, and forcibly curtailing their freedom can rescue them, there seem to be no reasons grounded in rights for not stepping in. Consider a man who spends all his salary drinking himself into a stupor every evening, ruining his health and driving away his wife and friends. Whatever the merits of a diurnal drunken stupor in lonely splendor, they don't add up to furthering his capacity for free agency. On what grounds, then, could a theory that sees rights as promoting this capacity say that such a man has a right to freedom from forcible paternalistic interference? That the only recourse with such a man is rational argument, appeals to his better self, tough love,

or psychological manipulation by family and friends? One reason such a theory could give for the alcoholic's right to live an
inebriated life is that an individual must live his life by his own
efforts, that neither the state nor anyone else, no matter how
well-intentioned or wise, can do this for him. The state and
other individuals can, indeed, provide the alcoholic with external goods, but not with the self-direction he so sorely needs.

In a sense, of course, this is completely true. It is a necessary
truth that no one can force another to be self-directed because
this precludes being forced by another. However, it does not
follow, nor is there any reason to believe, that forcible interference can never play a causal role in setting an individual on the
path of self-direction. Forcible interference often plays this role
in the moral education of children and adolescents, and it can
do so in the case of adults who are in the grip of addiction.
Thus, if rights exist to further the capacity for agency, then no
one has a right to undermine his own agency, and neither other
individuals nor the state have a principled reason to refrain from
paternalistic interference. There may, indeed, be other reasons
for refraining—reasons of fallibility, the slippery slope of state
power, and so on—but not a reason grounded in rights.

To summarize: When rights are construed as furthering
agency, even the individualist maxim that it is rational for us to
seek our own good cannot provide a principled barrier to paternalism or to being used as a mere means to the ends of others.
In other words, the fundamental rights to liberty cannot be
justified as furthering the value of free agency. But it is a mistake
to think that valuing something is always a matter of furthering
it, whether that something is persons and their rights or other
values that have an intrinsic (and not merely instrumental) importance, such as friendship, truth, knowledge, and virtue. In
each case, the conception of value as that which must be pro-

moted fails to capture the full value of the item in question.[10] This other dimension is captured only when we recognize that we also value things by *honoring* them or *appreciating* them. In the next section I argue that rights can perform the task of creating a space of protected freedom for individuals only if they are seen as reflecting this sort of valuing response to individuals.

3. HONORING FREE AGENCY

Things that are ends in themselves, that is, things that have intrinsic value, call not only for protection or promotion but also for *appreciation*. Art objects and other objects of beauty are obvious examples of such things. Attention to the aesthetic properties of things, the properties that make them things of beauty, evokes a valuing response that says, in effect, that it is

10. This point was first made by Robert Nozick when he distinguished between two sorts of moral theories, those that see all moral concerns as goals or end-states to be promoted and those that see some moral concerns as calling for side constraints (*Anarchy, State, and Utopia* [New York: Basic Books, 1974], 28–33). He argues that the former can support only a utilitarianism of rights and thus cannot sufficiently respect persons as distinct individuals. Nevertheless, arguments for rights that implicitly or explicitly take an end-state view of value have continued to be made even by those who take themselves to be rejecting utilitarianism. See also Eric Mack's argument against these theories in "In Defense of the Jurisdiction Theory of Rights," *Journal of Ethics* 3, nos. 1–2 (2000): 71–98.

The general point that not all value is not something to be promoted has since been made by the following authors in different ways: Michael Stocker, "Values and Purposes: The Limits of Teleology and the Ends of Friendship," *Journal of Philosophy* 78 (1981): 747–65; Christine Korsgaard, "The Reasons We Can Share: An Attack on the Distinction Between Agent-Relative and Agent-Neutral Values," *Creating the Kingdom of Ends* (Cambridge: Harvard University Press, 1996), 275–310; Christine Swanton, "Profiles of the Virtues," *Pacific Philosophical Quarterly* 76 (1995): 47–72; Velleman and Neera Badhwar Kapur, "Why It's Wrong to be Always Guided by the Best: Friendship and Consequentialism," *Ethics* (April 1991): 483–504.

good that they exist—good not for this or that purpose but simply for what they are. A sunset over the Grand Canyon, a Rodin sculpture, a cherry tree in blossom—all add value to the lives of those who perceive them. Many of the discoveries and innovations of human intellect and enterprise, in addition to being valued for their utility, also evoke this kind of appreciation. A mathematical theorem, a bread machine that turns out perfectly shaped loaves, a sleek, noiseless train—all can be objects of aesthetic appreciation by virtue of their sheer cleverness and ingenuity. And appreciation is free of any urge to do something to or for the object of appreciation; it consists simply of the inclination to stand back and look, in pleasure or admiration or reverence.

If these products of human interest and energy and creativity are worthy objects of appreciation, how much more worthy, then, are persons, who both create and appreciate these products. Unlike other living entities, we not only seek or pursue that which is of value to us, as the sunflower seeks the sun or the tiger pursues its prey, but we also create it. And unlike the sunflower or the tiger, we not only use what is of instrumental value to us, but we also value it, that is, perceive it as an instrumental value. Depending on the object, we can also appreciate it as an end in itself. Indeed, with sufficient imagination, we can appreciate even the most mundane of things, from the design of a toothbrush to the multicolored variety of rubber bands in a stationery store. And this exercise of the capacity for valuation is a kind of creation as well, insofar as it bestows value on things by attending to them and realizing their potential to surprise and delight in ever new ways. Persons, and persons alone, appreciate value and create value, including even the value of their own individual lives. This is what makes individuals the owners of their own lives. And this is why human agency is the ground of dignity and why individuals are worthy objects of not only appreciation but also a special kind of appreciation, which we may mark by calling "honor."

It is respect construed as honor that inclines one to stand back and look rather than to protect or promote that reflects the status of individuals as being equal in their capacity to value and to create value. To appreciate persons for themselves is to honor them for their power of valuation and creation, a power that gives them a godlike authority over their own lives. In respecting individuals, we give priority to their status as agents rather than as potential recipients of benefits, as beings with sovereignty over their own lives who must therefore be left alone to direct their lives as they deem fit.

To see individuals as equally sovereign is to see both that using them as mere means to others' ends is to devalue them and that they are free, if they wish, to sacrifice themselves for the good of others. In addition, to see individuals as sovereign is to see both that trying to further their good against their will is to devalue and violate them and that they are free, if they wish, to seek help from others. When valuing individuals as agents is seen entirely as a matter of protecting and promoting their agency, it is impossible to understand why Dax Cowart, who was forced to endure months of agonizing treatment despite repeated pleas to be allowed to die, should even now be convinced that he was not given the respect due to him, that forcing treatment on him violated his rights.[11] It is impossible to understand this because although permanently disfigured and blinded, Cowart retained his ability to direct his life and, indeed, now leads a productive, worthwhile, happy life.

What, then, is the attitude of those who honor their *own* status as ends? Most obviously, it requires that they not see

11. Jennifer Stump, "Cowart to appear on *20/20:* Local Lawyer Fights for Patients' Rights" (*Corpus Christi Online*, March 22, 1999).

themselves as mere means to others' ends, tools for their use. This is how the slave who internalizes his master's perspective sees himself in relation to his master. This is also how the deferential wife sees herself in relation to her husband. And in seeing themselves thus, what the slave and the wife both fail to do is value themselves as the proper "final causes" of their actions, the objects for the sake of which and in honor of which they may properly act. The only proper final causes, the only ends worth acting for and worth honoring, in their estimation, are superior others. Hence, too, it is these others and not they themselves who are the efficient causes, the initiators, of their actions. Their wills belong to another. Those who see themselves as ends, then, see themselves as the proper final and efficient causes of their actions, the prime movers of their lives. In acknowledging their own value, they pay heed to themselves, give themselves proper attention. Likewise, if they also respect others, they recognize them as proper final causes of their own actions and the prime movers of their own lives. Rights are the principled, public recognition of this fact of personhood.

Rights, in Eric Mack's words, are "jurisdictional claims over particular segments of the world," giving to the right-holder the moral power to determine how she will use her physical and mental faculties.[12] Others may not use her to benefit themselves or others because, as Robert Nozick puts it, she is a distinct individual with her "*own* life to lead."[13] Likewise, neither the state nor other individuals may coerce her for her own good because she is a distinct individual with her "own life to *lead*."[14] Rights construed as jurisdictional claims provide a principled barrier to paternalism because they give the right-holder the

---

12. Mack, "In Defense of the Jurisdiction Theory of Rights," 95.
13. Nozick, *Anarchy, State, and Utopia*, 34.
14. Ibid.

moral power to live wisely or unwisely. Wanting rights for oneself and respecting others' rights is the appropriate response to one's own and others' inviolability.

Mutual respect for rights, then, reflects a mutual honoring of each others' normative status as agents. Unlike the agency-furthering defense, this agency-honoring defense leaves no possibility that the same facts about us—our agency—that give rise to rights and justify respect for them will also justify their violation for the sake of preventing more violations or for furthering the agent's own good. For the ground is simply that we are the sort of beings who are both the final causes and the prime movers of our actions, and this fact calls on us to refrain from interference.

However, this defense of rights does not imply that rights are always trumps, that is, that we must respect rights at any cost, putting them above all other moral principles or values. Not only can moral principles and values conflict, but so also can principles of rationality. Hence, in some cases there may be no univocal—or any—rational answer to the question of what is the right act. An act of rights-respecting justice can destroy an individual's well-being, even when his conception of well-being entails the disposition to respect others' rights.[15] And reason does not tell us that in the event of such a conflict, respect for rights must always trump concern for one's own well-being—or the other way around. Much would depend on the right in question and the effect on the rights-bearer of violating it. For example, making a false promise to meet a friend for dinner

---

15. This is paradoxical, but it is not incoherent. The thought is that well-being requires the virtue of justice, but, nevertheless, a particular act of justice can lead (for example) to a reprisal that ruins an individual's well-being. This is analogous to saying that good health requires regular exercise but that a particular act of exercising can lead to an accident that ruins an individual's health.

in order to shake a would-be killer off one's track seems obviously right if the act does not thereby endanger the friend's life—and obviously wrong if it does. And no friend—or any decent human being—would want one to do any differently in the former case. Indeed, in such a case, any decent individual would retroactively waive the right to one's promise-keeping, just as that individual would expect one to waive one's right if the situation was reversed.

Again, reason does not give a univocal answer when there is a conflict between respecting others' rights and preventing a gross violation of one's own rights or the rights of those one loves or admires for their exceptional character or achievements. This problem can be put in sharper focus if we imagine that the individual whose rights are in question is suspected of being violent. Although one does not have a right to violate anyone's rights to prevent violations of one's own or someone else's rights, one may well have reasons of both justice and benevolence to do just that, for example, on behalf of someone under our care. At the same time, because it is at best excusable but never right to violate someone's rights, one owes the suspect compensation if one does violate his rights.

So far the discussion has focused on cases where individuals may be excused for violating someone's rights. Insofar as the excusing circumstances are considerations of friendship or virtue, they do not apply to the state. Yet one can think of cases in times of war or natural catastrophe when the state might have an excuse for violating some people's rights to prevent an even graver violation of other people's rights.

Unlike both the agency-promotion view and utilitarian views, the agency-honoring view yields rights against trade-offs between individuals as well as against forcible paternalistic interference, regardless of the external circumstances. What it does not, because it cannot, do is say that rights must be trumps over all other considerations.

In this conflict of reasons and values, we are confronted not with what Henry Sidgwick called "the Dualism of Practical Reason" (the conflict between the principle of benevolence and the principle of self-interest)[16] but with the multiplicity of practical reason. And this has to do not with the limitations of our understanding but with the plurality of values in a world of contingencies.

At the same time, however, this plurality also gives us a plurality of reasons for respecting others' rights. Because rights do generally serve to further our own and others' good, and respect for others' rights is generally in our own interest for both instrumental and noninstrumental reasons, we have more than one reason for wanting rights for ourselves and for respecting others' rights.

4. ARE RIGHTS TOO WESTERN?

I have assumed throughout that the concept of persons as valuers and creators of value is universal, hence that rights are universally valid. But are they? Rights have been challenged from many directions. As L. W. Sumner states:

> Marxists may find rights too bourgeois, conservatives may find them too liberal, communitarians may find them too individualistic, Europeans may find them too American, and consequentialists may find them too deontological.[17]

One may add to this list: Asians and Africans may find them too

16. Henry Sidgwick, *The Methods of Ethics*, 7th ed. (London: Macmillian, 1907), 404, 506–9.
17. L. W. Summer, *The Moral Foundations of Rights* (Oxford: Clarendon Press, 1987), 9.

Western. Is the concept of fundamental equal rights a parochial concept? Is there any merit to the protests of many leaders and thinkers in Asian and African countries that the concept is alien to Asian and African values? We need not worry too much when the leaders of dictatorships like China or Burma complain that they have their "own" conception of democracy and human rights—especially when they add that on this conception "individuals must put the state's rights before their own."[18] This is merely a secular counterpart of the traditional claim of the Divine Right of Kings (though embodied in a form of politics wholly original in the extent of its control of the individual). But we can still ask if the concept of rights has a basis in the ethical and political ideals of non-Western systems of thought.

That respect for rights was not a widespread political ideal in any non-Western country before colonization by Great Britain and other Western countries is undeniable. But neither was it a widespread political ideal in the West before the Enlightenment: socioeconomic hierarchies supported and were supported by political hierarchies. However, what was largely absent in pre-Enlightenment Europe, and what is still absent from most Asian and African countries, is not the idea of the right to live one's life as one chooses but rather the idea that this right does not belong exclusively to the few who are "naturally" or politically superior. The politically powerful have always arro-

18. Quoted in Amartya Sen, "Human Rights and Asian Values" (New York: Carnegie Council on Ethics and International Affairs, 1997). This comment by the spokesman of China's foreign ministry was perhaps the most noteworthy of the comments made at the World Conference on Human Rights in Vienna in June 1993. Others included Premier Li Peng of China's declaration that "[t]he imposition of a certain conception of democracy and human rights should be opposed," and the Foreign Ministry Official of Burma's statement that "[t]he Asian countries, with their own norms and standards of human rights, should not be dictated to . . . " (*Time*, June 28, 1993).

gated this right to themselves. In other words, what was and is still largely missing is the idea of the moral equality of all individuals. Yet, as Sen points out, even some Asian countries have had regimes in which moral equality and equal rights were recognized in at least some spheres of life.[19] India is noteworthy here with its long history of regimes that had policies of religious tolerance, especially in the third century B.C. under Emperor Ashoka and in the sixteenth century A.D. under the Moghul Emperor Akbar.

Again, although no strong rights tradition existed in the West before the Enlightenment and no rights tradition has ever existed in many Asian countries, the idea of the equal moral worth of all moral agents is present in much of the religious or philosophical thought of those cultures: the Confucianism of Mencius, some variants of Islam and Hinduism, Buddhism, Judaism, and, of course, Christianity.[20] Thus, Mencius holds that all agents have the capacity for virtue (the "sprouts" of the four basic virtues) and sees respect for self and others as a central part of the virtue of righteousness.[21] For example, he writes that it is wrong to use contemptuous forms of address or give alms to a beggar with contempt. Any righteous person will refuse such forms of address, and the righteous beggar will refuse alms given in this spirit. Similarly, a wife or concubine should be ashamed of a husband or lover who humiliates himself for material gain, and people should disdain to serve base rulers. In all these cases, what is at issue is the equal dignity of all.

According to Mencius, then, everyone is equal in the capacity for goodness, and even those on the lowest rung of the social

19. Sen, "Human Rights and Asian Values," 19–25.
20. Albert Weale, "Equality," *Routledge Encyclopaedia of Philosophy* (online version, 2000).
21. Bryan W. Van Norden, "Mencius," *Routledge Encyclopaedia of Philosophy* (1998).

order have a capacity for self-respect and are deserving of others' respect. There is nothing particularly Western, then, in the idea of equal moral worth. What is Western is its wide acceptance and firm entrenchment in the politics and political theory of the West. And what made it possible was the growing realization of people that their sense of the inevitability of the social and political hierarchies to which they belonged was itself the result of these hierarchies[22]—precisely the realization that those who decry individual rights wish to block.

5. CONCLUSION

I have argued that our equal moral worth as moral agents lies in our capacity for valuing and creating: valuing this capacity and its worthy manifestations in ourselves and others and creating worthy selves and objects. It is this capacity that confers *dignity* on all moral agents, a value to which the proper response is appreciation or honor. Rights to liberty are the moral and legal expressions of honor for individuals as separate and distinct persons with their own lives to lead. I have also argued that this notion of persons exists in many Asian philosophies and religions. The absence of legally recognized rights to liberty in these countries, then, cannot be traced to different underlying values, as their leaders claim, but simply to the leaders' unwillingness to honor the status of their citizens as free and equal individuals.

22. Bernard Williams, "The Idea of Equality," *Problems of the Self* (Cambridge: Cambridge University Press, 1973), 238–39.

INDEX

Congress, 67, 82. *See also* United
 States
consent to be governed
 ambiguities in the, 62–63
 Americans', 62
Constitution (U.S.)
 antidemocratic nature of, 75–76
 Article 2 of, 76
 erosion of, 78
 v. the federal government, 77–78
 First Amendment of, 75
 as Founding Father's limitation on
  government, 81–82
 "general welfare" clause of, 78–79
 habeas corpus of, 76, 85
 importance of America's, 73
 interstate commerce and, 78
 Lockean influence on, 3
 rights of man in, 84, 85
 Second Amendment of, 75, 85. *See
  also* Bill of Rights (U.S.);
  Founding Fathers (U.S.); United
  States
Constitutional Convention of 1787.
 See Founding Fathers (U.S.);
 United States
constitutions in republics, 73
contemporary republicanism, 14*n*7
Cowart, Dax, 108, 108*n*11
Cowen, Martin L., III, 48*n*13
Curren, Randall R., 36*n*6

Declaration of Independence, xiv–xv,
 75, 91
 Lockean influence on, 3
 vagueness of rights of man in, 82–
  87
deliberative democracy, 14*n*7
democracies, large
 difficulties of voting in, 67, 69
 difficulty of handling details in,
  67–68
 judiciary power in, 69
 loss of democracy in, 67–69

necessity of creating bureaucracies
 in, 68
democracy
 advent over aristocracy of, xvii
 anarchistic, xxi–xxii, xxii*n*9
 aristocracy v., xvii, 4–5, 45–46
 Benjamin Barber's strong, 14*n*7
 deliberative, 14*n*7
 different views of, xiii
 elections and, 65–66
 ethics v., xiv
 governmental shakeup in, 4
 idealism v. realism and, 3
 indirect, 67–69
 justice and, xxi–xxiii
 legal system's dependency on, xxi–
  xxii
 liberty v., 3
 limiting the scope of, xxi–xxiv
 literal meaning of, xiii
 problems in instituting, 4, 13–14
 problems of a large, 67–68
 public goods' function of, 7
 redistribution of wealth and, xxii–
  xxv, xxiii*n*10, 22, 69–72, 79–
  80
 v. self-government, 64
 sphere of, xix. *See also* Aristotle;
  democracies, large; democracy,
  default; democracy, dynamic;
  democracy, expressive;
  democracy, justifications for;
  democracies, unlimited;
  democratic ideal; democratic
  politics
democracy, default, 4–9, 22, 25, 28
 defining, 5
 public choice theory and, 7–9, 24
democracy, dynamic, 9–18, 24
 achieving, 16–17
 as antidote to corporate control
  and bureaucracy, 16
 coercion of, 24
 defining, 9–15

Declaration of Independence of,
xiv–xv, 3, 75, 82–87, 91
the draft and, 85, 86–87
election and duties of presidents
in, 76–77
election frequency in, 65
Electoral College of, 76
"general welfare" of, 78–79
groups excluded from voting in,
66
House of Representatives of, 76
plurality of voting in, 65
Senate of, 76
Seventeenth Amendment of, 76
Supreme Court of, 69, 81, 82
as an unlimited democracy, xx, 79
wealth redistribution in, 79–80
World War II and, 86–87. *See also*
Founding Fathers (U.S.);
democracy; democracies, large

value, agent-relative, 94. *See also*
value, personal; moral worth,
equal
value, intrinsic
appreciation of objects with, 106–
7
utilitarian v., 107
value, personal, 98, 99.
impersonal v., 94–95
interpersonal comparisons, self-
regard, and, 96, 97
Silas Marner's life as example of
varying, 95–96. *See also* moral
worth, equal
valuing
furthering v., 105–6
self v. others, 108–9. *See also*
moral worth, equal
Velleman, J. David, 97, 97n6, 99n7
voluntariness, 63–64
ambiguities in, 63–64
brainwashing and, 63–64

coercion v., 63
influence and, 63
voting
different models for, 66–67
expressive value of, 21, 23
groups excluded from, 66
large democracies and difficulties
in, 67, 69
large democracies and
inconsequentiality of, 19–21,
23, 23n9, 25, 67, 68
morality and, 27
problems of anonymity in, 26, 28
problems of uninformed citizenry
in, 69–70

Walker, Kent, 102
Washington, D.C., 67
Washington, George, 74. *See also*
Founding Fathers (U.S.)
Weale, Albert, 114n20
wealth, redistribution of
democracy and, xxii–xxv,
xxiiin10, 22, 69–72, 79–80
Weimar Republic, xx
welfare states
growth of liberal democratic, 22
"will of the people, the"
acceptance of some checks on, xxii
determining, xiii–xvi, xivn2
Willard v. Filburn (1942), 78
Williams, Bernard, 93
Winthrop, Delba, 30n2
Wolin, Sheldon, 30, 30n2
World Conference on Human Rights
in Vienna (1993), 113n18
World War II
United States and, 86–87

Zaire, 8
Zimbabweans, 64
Zvesper, John, 31, 31n4

PHILOSOPHIC REFLECTIONS

ON A FREE SOCIETY

A Series Edited by Tibor R. Machan

Business Ethics in the Global Market

Education in a Free Society

Morality and Work

*Individual Rights Reconsidered: Are the Truths of
the U.S. Declaration of Independence Lasting?*

The Commons: Its Tragedies and Other Follies

Liberty and Equality

Liberty and Hard Cases

Liberty and Research and Development

Liberty and Democracy